Documented Paranormal Events

Shah Rukh

Published by Shah Rukh, 2024.

While every precaution has been taken in the preparation of this book, the publisher assumes no responsibility for errors or omissions, or for damages resulting from the use of the information contained herein.

DOCUMENTED PARANORMAL EVENTS

First edition. July 2, 2024.

Copyright © 2024 Shah Rukh.

Written by Shah Rukh.

Table of Contents

Prologue

For centuries, tales of the supernatural have captivated the human imagination. Whispers of ghostly apparitions, unexplained phenomena, and eerie encounters have woven themselves into the very fabric of our history. While many dismiss these stories as mere folklore or the result of overactive imaginations, there remains a wealth of documented evidence suggesting that something far more mysterious lies beyond the veil of our everyday reality.

This book, "Documented Paranormal Events," is a journey into the heart of the unknown. Each chapter delves into a unique and well-documented paranormal occurrence, carefully selected from various times and places. These stories are not the stuff of fiction; they are real events witnessed by real people, often leaving behind a trail of evidence that continues to baffle and intrigue.

In these pages, you will explore the haunted corridors of ancient castles, the spectral remnants of long-lost ships, and the chilling accounts of encounters with otherworldly beings. From the infamous Bell Witch haunting to the eerie legends of the Bermuda Triangle, each story presents a puzzle that challenges our understanding of the world.

Our journey begins in the early 19th century with the haunting of the Bell family in Tennessee and takes us through time and across continents, revealing the enduring nature of these mysterious phenomena. As you read, you will meet ordinary people who have experienced extraordinary events—people whose lives were forever changed by their brush with the supernatural.

Whether you are a skeptic seeking to understand the unexplained, a believer looking to delve deeper into the world of the paranormal, or simply a curious reader, this book offers a comprehensive and compelling look at some of history's most fascinating and bewildering cases.

Prepare to question what you know about reality. The stories within these pages will challenge your perceptions, stir your imagination, and perhaps even make you reconsider the nature of the world around you. Welcome to "Documented Paranormal Events"—a collection of true stories that remind us that sometimes, the most incredible tales are the ones that are true.

Chapter 1: The Haunting of the Bell Witch

The Haunting of the Bell Witch is one of the most famous and extensively documented paranormal events in American folklore. This mysterious phenomenon is said to have taken place in the early 19th century in the home of John Bell, a farmer who resided in Adams, Tennessee. The tale begins around 1817, when John Bell and his family started experiencing inexplicable events on their property. Initially, the disturbances were subtle—unusual noises such as knocking, scratching, and the sound of rats gnawing on furniture. However, these noises soon escalated to more overtly supernatural occurrences.

The Bell family reportedly heard disembodied voices, witnessed objects moving on their own, and experienced physical assaults by an unseen force. The entity, which came to be known as the Bell Witch, was particularly antagonistic towards John Bell and his daughter, Betsy. Betsy was subjected to violent physical attacks, including being slapped, pinched, and having her hair pulled by the invisible assailant. The Bell Witch's voice, described as shrill and raspy, frequently taunted and threatened the family, making it clear that it intended to harm John Bell.

As the haunting continued, the Bell Witch's notoriety spread, attracting the attention of neighbors, curious onlookers, and even notable figures. One of the most famous visitors to the Bell household was future President Andrew Jackson, who had heard tales of the haunting and wanted to witness the phenomena firsthand. According to legend, Jackson and his entourage experienced a terrifying night at the Bell farm, with Jackson reportedly declaring, "I would rather fight the entire British Army than to deal with the Bell Witch."

Despite numerous attempts to rid the household of the entity, including religious rites and exorcisms, the haunting persisted for years.

The Bell Witch's presence grew increasingly malevolent, culminating in the mysterious illness and eventual death of John Bell in 1820. On his deathbed, Bell is said to have been tormented by the witch, who claimed responsibility for his impending demise. After his death, the witch reportedly laughed and sang joyously.

One of the most intriguing aspects of the Bell Witch legend is the witch's stated motive. According to the lore, the witch identified herself as "Kate," a spirit seeking vengeance against John Bell for reasons that remain unclear. Some accounts suggest that Bell had wronged a neighbor named Kate Batts, leading to speculation that the witch was acting on her behalf. However, no definitive evidence supports this theory, and the true nature and origin of the Bell Witch remain shrouded in mystery.

Over time, the Bell Witch legend has become deeply embedded in American folklore, inspiring numerous books, films, and even a play. The story continues to capture the imagination of paranormal enthusiasts and skeptics alike, with many visiting Adams, Tennessee, to explore the site of the haunting. The Bell Witch Cave, a natural cave located near the old Bell farm, is a popular destination for those seeking to connect with the supernatural elements of the legend. Visitors to the cave have reported experiencing strange phenomena, such as hearing voices and feeling an unexplained sense of dread.

Skeptics have proposed various explanations for the Bell Witch phenomena, ranging from mass hysteria and psychological suggestion to outright fabrication. Some suggest that the disturbances were the result of natural causes, such as underground watercourses or seismic activity, which could have produced the strange sounds and vibrations reported by the Bell family. Others believe that the haunting was a hoax perpetrated by members of the Bell family or their neighbors for reasons that remain speculative.

Despite these theories, the Bell Witch haunting remains one of the most compelling and enduring stories of the supernatural in American history. It serves as a potent reminder of the power of folklore and the human fascination with the unknown. The tale of the Bell Witch continues to be told and retold, each generation adding its own embellishments and interpretations to the legend. Whether viewed as a cautionary tale, a piece of cultural heritage, or a genuine account of paranormal activity, the story of the Bell Witch endures as a testament to the enduring power of mystery and fear.

Chapter 2: The Enfield Poltergeist

The Enfield Poltergeist is one of the most infamous and well-documented cases of purported poltergeist activity, capturing the public's imagination and fueling debates among paranormal enthusiasts and skeptics alike. The events took place in the London borough of Enfield, England, primarily involving a single-parent family consisting of Peggy Hodgson and her four children: Margaret, Janet, Johnny, and Billy. The disturbances began in August 1977 and continued for a period of 18 months, drawing significant media attention and investigation from both paranormal researchers and the press.

The haunting began on the evening of August 30, 1977, when Peggy Hodgson reported that she heard strange noises coming from her daughters' bedroom. Upon investigation, she found Janet and Margaret visibly distressed, claiming that their beds were shaking and objects were moving on their own. Over the next few days, the incidents escalated, with furniture being overturned, knocking sounds echoing throughout the house, and objects being thrown across rooms without any apparent cause. The family initially believed that there might be an intruder or that they were the victims of a prank, but as the events continued, they became convinced that something supernatural was at play.

The phenomena soon attracted the attention of neighbors and local authorities. Police officers who responded to the Hodgson's calls for help witnessed some of the activity themselves, including a chair moving across the floor without any visible means of propulsion. Unable to offer an explanation, they suggested the family contact the Society for Psychical Research (SPR), a prominent organization dedicated to investigating paranormal phenomena. Among the investigators who took an interest in the case were Maurice Grosse and Guy Lyon Playfair, both of whom spent considerable time at the

Hodgson home, documenting the occurrences and interviewing the family members.

Grosse and Playfair reported experiencing a wide range of phenomena, including inexplicable knocking sounds, furniture moving, and even the physical levitation of Janet, the 11-year-old daughter who appeared to be at the center of much of the activity. Janet was also seen speaking in a deep, gravelly voice that she claimed was not her own but that of a spirit named "Bill." This voice often communicated disturbing messages, claiming to be a former resident of the house who had died there. Recordings of these sessions with Janet provided some of the most compelling and eerie evidence of the alleged haunting.

The investigators used various methods to try to capture evidence of the poltergeist activity, including setting up cameras and recording equipment throughout the house. Photographs taken during the investigation purportedly show Janet being thrown from her bed and other objects in mid-air. These images, along with audio recordings of the strange voices and knocking sounds, were presented as evidence of the poltergeist's presence. The case received widespread media coverage, with newspapers and television programs featuring interviews with the Hodgson family and the investigators, further heightening public interest in the haunting.

Despite the compelling nature of the evidence presented by Grosse, Playfair, and the media, the Enfield Poltergeist case has been the subject of considerable skepticism. Critics argue that many of the phenomena could have been fabricated or exaggerated, pointing to instances where Janet and her siblings were caught bending spoons and other objects in an attempt to simulate paranormal activity. Some skeptics suggest that the entire case was a hoax perpetrated by the Hodgson children, possibly as a means of seeking attention or as a reaction to the stresses of their home life. The fact that some of the activity seemed to subside when the children were not present lends credence to this theory.

However, those who support the authenticity of the Enfield Poltergeist case argue that the sheer volume and consistency of the reported phenomena, as well as the involvement of credible witnesses such as police officers and independent investigators, make it unlikely that the entire affair was a fabrication. They point out that while some incidents could be attributed to trickery, others defy simple explanation and suggest a genuine paranormal presence. The involvement of multiple witnesses who had no apparent motive to deceive adds weight to the argument that something extraordinary was occurring in the Hodgson home.

In the years since the Enfield Poltergeist case, it has become one of the most studied and debated instances of supposed paranormal activity. It has been the subject of numerous books, documentaries, and even a feature film, "The Conjuring 2," which dramatizes the events with a degree of artistic license. The case continues to fascinate those interested in the supernatural, serving as both a cautionary tale about the dangers of taking such reports at face value and a tantalizing glimpse into the possibility of otherworldly phenomena.

The legacy of the Enfield Poltergeist case is multifaceted, impacting the fields of parapsychology, media, and popular culture. For parapsychologists, it represents a complex and challenging case that defies easy categorization, offering both tantalizing evidence of paranormal activity and frustrating ambiguities. For the media, it highlights the powerful allure of ghost stories and the potential for such tales to capture the public's imagination. And for popular culture, the Enfield Poltergeist remains a potent source of inspiration, a modern-day ghost story that continues to be retold and reinterpreted.

Despite the passage of time and the ongoing debates about the veracity of the events, the Enfield Poltergeist case endures as one of the most compelling narratives in the annals of paranormal research. Whether viewed as a genuine encounter with the unknown or a complex psychological and social phenomenon, it challenges our understanding of reality and the limits of human perception. The case invites us to consider the possibility that there are forces beyond our comprehension, lurking at the edges of our understanding, waiting to be glimpsed in moments of fear and uncertainty.

Chapter 3: The Mystery of the Mary Celeste

The Mystery of the Mary Celeste remains one of the most enduring maritime enigmas, captivating the imagination of people for over a century. The Mary Celeste was a brigantine merchant ship found adrift and deserted in the Atlantic Ocean on December 4, 1872, by the Canadian brigantine Dei Gratia. The ship was in good condition and fully provisioned, yet the crew had vanished without a trace, leaving behind a mystery that has never been conclusively solved.

The Mary Celeste set sail from New York City on November 7, 1872, bound for Genoa, Italy, carrying a cargo of 1,701 barrels of denatured alcohol. The ship was captained by Benjamin Briggs, an experienced and respected mariner. Onboard were his wife, Sarah, their two-year-old daughter, Sophia, and a crew of seven, making a total of ten people. The crew was carefully selected by Briggs, and all were considered reliable and experienced sailors.

On December 4, the Dei Gratia, commanded by Captain David Morehouse, sighted the Mary Celeste approximately 400 miles east of the Azores. Observing that the ship was sailing erratically, Morehouse sent a boarding party to investigate. Upon boarding, the crew of the Dei Gratia found the Mary Celeste deserted. The ship's single lifeboat was missing, as were the ship's papers, except for the captain's logbook. The last entry in the log was dated November 25, nine days earlier, and indicated nothing amiss. The ship was seaworthy, with the cargo largely intact and sufficient provisions to last for six months. The personal belongings of the crew and passengers, including valuables, were undisturbed.

Several theories have been proposed over the years to explain the disappearance of the Mary Celeste's crew. One of the earliest theories suggested that the crew abandoned ship due to an explosion or the fear of an explosion caused by the cargo of alcohol. Some of the barrels were found to be empty, leading to speculation that leaking fumes might have caused an explosion or made the crew fear one was imminent. However, there were no signs of fire or explosion damage on the ship.

Another theory posits that a sudden seaquake or waterspout could have caused the crew to panic and abandon ship. A seaquake could have generated violent waves, causing the crew to believe the ship was in immediate danger of sinking. Similarly, a waterspout could have created a temporary but terrifying situation, prompting a hasty evacuation. However, this does not explain why the crew would have left a seaworthy vessel with ample provisions and not returned once the immediate threat had passed.

Mutiny and piracy have also been suggested as explanations. The theory of mutiny involves the crew rising up against Captain Briggs and abandoning ship, though no evidence supports this scenario. Additionally, the absence of struggle signs or violence aboard the Mary Celeste makes this theory less likely. The idea of piracy also lacks evidence, as the ship's cargo and valuables were untouched.

Some have speculated that the crew fell victim to foul play by the crew of the Dei Gratia. However, this theory is weakened by the fact that Captain Morehouse and Briggs were acquaintances, and the Dei Gratia crew would have had little to gain from such an act, especially considering the high risk involved in orchestrating and covering up such a crime.

A more fantastical theory involves paranormal activity or extraterrestrial intervention. While these ideas are popular in fiction and among conspiracy theorists, they lack any empirical evidence and are generally dismissed by serious researchers.

The condition of the ship when discovered offers some clues but no definitive answers. The sails were partially set and in poor condition, some rigging was damaged, and there was a slight amount of water between decks, but nothing to suggest an immediate and overwhelming danger. The ship's pumps were operational, and the cargo hold contained several feet of water, but this was not unusual for a vessel of its age and type.

The disappearance of the Mary Celeste's crew has been the subject of numerous investigations, books, and fictional accounts, each offering different interpretations and embellishments. Despite exhaustive research and analysis, the true fate of the crew remains unknown, and the mystery endures.

In 1884, Arthur Conan Doyle, the creator of Sherlock Holmes, published a short story titled "J. Habakuk Jephson's Statement," which fictionalized the Mary Celeste incident and introduced elements that have become intertwined with the mythos of the ship. Doyle's story, although fictional, popularized many misconceptions and added to the intrigue surrounding the case.

Modern investigations have revisited the case with advanced techniques, but no new evidence has emerged to provide a definitive explanation. The mystery of the Mary Celeste continues to fascinate, embodying the allure of the unknown and the sea's vast, unforgiving nature. Theories range from plausible to outlandish, but none can conclusively explain why a well-provisioned, seaworthy ship was found adrift without its crew.

The legacy of the Mary Celeste is a testament to the enduring power of mystery and the human drive to seek answers, even when they remain elusive. The story of the Mary Celeste serves as a reminder of the unpredictable and often perilous nature of life at sea, and the many unknowns that still lie beneath the surface of our world's oceans.

Chapter 4: The Amityville Horror

The Amityville Horror is one of the most infamous and controversial stories of paranormal activity in American history. The tale begins with a horrific crime that occurred on November 13, 1974, in the quiet suburban town of Amityville, located on Long Island, New York. On that night, 23-year-old Ronald DeFeo Jr. shot and killed six members of his family: his father Ronald DeFeo Sr., his mother Louise, and his four siblings, Dawn, Allison, Marc, and John Matthew, while they slept in their beds. DeFeo later confessed to the murders, claiming that voices in the house had urged him to commit the crime. He was subsequently convicted of the murders and sentenced to life in prison.

The house at 112 Ocean Avenue, where the murders took place, was a large, Dutch Colonial-style home with distinctive quarter-moon windows. Despite its grim history, the house did not remain vacant for long. In December 1975, just over a year after the murders, George and Kathy Lutz purchased the home for a remarkably low price of $80,000. The Lutzes, along with Kathy's three children from a previous marriage, moved into the house, hoping to start a new chapter in their lives. However, they would soon claim that their new home was haunted by a malevolent presence.

According to the Lutzes, their ordeal began almost immediately after moving in. They reported a series of increasingly disturbing paranormal events that made life in the house unbearable. The Lutzes claimed to have experienced strange and inexplicable phenomena, such as foul odors, cold spots, and mysterious green slime oozing from the walls. George Lutz reported waking up at 3:15 a.m. every night, the same time the DeFeo murders were believed to have occurred. He also claimed to have seen a demonic pig-like creature with glowing red eyes staring into the house from outside.

The Lutz family also experienced physical disturbances. Kathy Lutz claimed that she was levitated and unable to move while sleeping, and her children were said to have been repeatedly attacked by unseen forces. The family dog, Harry, reportedly exhibited signs of extreme fear, often cowering and refusing to enter certain areas of the house. Doors and windows were said to open and close on their own, and there were reports of eerie, disembodied voices.

After only 28 days, the Lutz family fled the house, leaving all their belongings behind. Their story quickly garnered media attention, and the Amityville Horror became a nationwide sensation. In 1977, Jay Anson published a book titled "The Amityville Horror," which purported to tell the true story of the Lutz family's experiences. The book became a bestseller and was later adapted into a successful film in 1979, spawning a franchise of sequels, remakes, and spin-offs.

Despite its popularity, the Amityville Horror story has been the subject of much skepticism and controversy. Critics argue that the Lutzes fabricated their story for financial gain, pointing to inconsistencies in their accounts and the lack of physical evidence to support their claims. Some have suggested that the family's experiences could be attributed to psychological factors, such as the traumatic history of the house and the power of suggestion.

Ronald DeFeo Jr., who was serving his life sentence at the time the Lutzes lived in the house, dismissed their story as a hoax. DeFeo's attorney, William Weber, later claimed that he, along with the Lutzes, had concocted the haunting story over several bottles of wine in an attempt to profit from the notoriety of the murders. Weber's admission further fueled skepticism about the authenticity of the Lutzes' claims.

Paranormal investigators Ed and Lorraine Warren, known for their work on other high-profile hauntings, were among those who believed in the validity of the Amityville haunting. The Warrens conducted an investigation of the house in 1976 and claimed to have experienced and documented evidence of paranormal activity. Lorraine Warren, a self-described clairvoyant, reported sensing a demonic presence in the house, and the Warrens presented photographs that they claimed showed ghostly figures.

Skeptics have countered these claims by pointing out that many of the Warrens' methods and findings lack scientific rigor and that their involvement may have been motivated by a desire to bolster their own reputations. Additionally, subsequent owners of the house have reported no paranormal activity, leading some to conclude that the Lutzes' story was a fabrication.

Despite the controversy, the Amityville Horror continues to be a compelling and influential part of American folklore. The house at 112 Ocean Avenue remains a popular subject of interest for paranormal enthusiasts and tourists, although the address has since been changed to deter curious onlookers. The story has inspired a vast array of books, movies, and documentaries, each offering different interpretations and embellishments of the Lutzes' experiences.

The enduring fascination with the Amityville Horror can be attributed to several factors. The combination of a gruesome true crime and a purportedly haunted house creates a compelling narrative that taps into deep-seated fears about the unknown and the possibility of evil forces at work in the world. The story also resonates with broader cultural themes, such as the American dream gone awry, the fragility of domestic life, and the thin boundary between reality and the supernatural.

In examining the Amityville Horror, it is important to consider the role of media and storytelling in shaping public perception. The sensational nature of the story, coupled with its widespread dissemination through books and films, has cemented its place in popular culture. The line between fact and fiction has become blurred, with each retelling adding new layers to the mythos of the haunted house.

Ultimately, the Amityville Horror remains an unsolved mystery, a modern legend that continues to captivate and provoke debate.

Whether viewed as a genuine paranormal event, a psychological phenomenon, or an elaborate hoax, the story challenges our understanding of the boundaries between the natural and the supernatural. It invites us to question what we believe and why, and to consider the power of fear and imagination in shaping our perceptions of the world around us.

Chapter 5: The Exorcism of Anneliese Michel

The exorcism of Anneliese Michel is one of the most controversial and tragic cases of purported demonic possession and exorcism in modern history. Anneliese Michel was born on September 21, 1952, in Leiblfing, Bavaria, Germany, to a devoutly Roman Catholic family. Her life was relatively normal until she began experiencing unusual and disturbing symptoms during her teenage years.

At the age of 16, Anneliese experienced her first epileptic seizure, which led to a diagnosis of temporal lobe epilepsy. Temporal lobe epilepsy is a neurological condition that can cause seizures, memory disturbances, and hallucinations. Despite being prescribed medication, Anneliese continued to suffer from seizures and began to experience other symptoms, including depression, which led her to seek psychiatric help. Over the next few years, Anneliese's condition worsened, despite various treatments and medications.

In addition to her medical and psychological symptoms, Anneliese began to exhibit behaviors that her deeply religious family interpreted as signs of demonic possession. She reportedly saw demonic faces, heard voices condemning her to hell, and became intolerant of religious objects and places. These symptoms intensified, and Anneliese's behavior became increasingly erratic and violent. She would exhibit extreme physical strength, scream for hours, destroy religious symbols, and refuse to eat, claiming that the demons would not allow her to consume food.

Convinced that their daughter was possessed by evil spirits, Anneliese's parents sought the help of the Catholic Church. They approached various priests, requesting an exorcism, but were initially turned down. The Church, adhering to strict guidelines and skepticism regarding claims of possession, recommended that Anneliese continue with medical treatment. However, as Anneliese's condition continued to deteriorate, her parents persisted in their quest for spiritual intervention.

Finally, in 1975, two priests, Father Arnold Renz and Father Ernst Alt, were granted permission by the local bishop to perform the rite of exorcism on Anneliese Michel. Over the course of ten months, from 1975 to 1976, a total of 67 exorcism sessions were conducted, each lasting up to four hours. These sessions were intended to expel the supposed demonic entities inhabiting Anneliese's body. During the exorcisms, Anneliese endured extreme physical and mental anguish, often screaming, contorting her body, and speaking in voices that were described as not her own.

Throughout the exorcism sessions, Anneliese's health continued to decline. She suffered from severe malnutrition and dehydration, as she often refused to eat or drink, believing that it was part of the demonic influence. Her physical condition became increasingly frail, and she exhibited signs of severe psychological distress. Despite the apparent lack of improvement, the exorcisms persisted, driven by the belief that Anneliese was being tormented by multiple demons, including Lucifer, Judas Iscariot, Nero, and Hitler.

On July 1, 1976, Anneliese Michel died in her home. She was 23 years old. The official cause of death was malnutrition and dehydration. At the time of her death, she weighed only 68 pounds. Her death sparked a criminal investigation and legal proceedings that brought the case to international attention. Anneliese's parents and the two priests who conducted the exorcisms were charged with negligent homicide. The trial, which began in 1978, attracted significant media coverage and public interest.

During the trial, the defense argued that Anneliese Michel had been possessed and that the exorcisms were a legitimate, albeit unsuccessful, attempt to save her. They presented recordings of the exorcism sessions as evidence, which included disturbing audio of

Anneliese's screams and voices. The prosecution, however, contended that Anneliese had been a mentally ill young woman who needed medical intervention rather than religious rites. They argued that the actions of her parents and the priests amounted to gross negligence, leading to her death from malnutrition and dehydration.

The court found Anneliese's parents and the priests guilty of negligent homicide. They were sentenced to six months in prison, which was later suspended, and three years of probation. The case raised important questions about the intersection of religion, mental health, and legal responsibility. It also highlighted the potential dangers of relying on religious rituals in place of medical treatment for mental illness.

The exorcism of Anneliese Michel continues to be a topic of intense debate and analysis. Some view Anneliese as a victim of religious fanaticism and a failure of the medical and legal systems to protect a vulnerable individual. Others believe that her case is a genuine instance of demonic possession and a testament to the power of faith and the spiritual realm. The story has inspired numerous books, documentaries, and films, including the 2005 movie "The Exorcism of Emily Rose," which dramatizes the events surrounding Anneliese's life and death.

From a psychological and medical perspective, Anneliese Michel's case can be seen as an example of the severe consequences of untreated or inadequately treated mental illness. Temporal lobe epilepsy, combined with her devout religious background, may have contributed to her belief that she was possessed. Her condition might have been exacerbated by a combination of neurological, psychological, and cultural factors, leading to a tragic outcome.

The case also underscores the importance of distinguishing between medical and spiritual issues. While religious beliefs and practices can provide comfort and support, they should not replace evidence-based medical treatments for mental and physical health conditions. The tragic fate of Anneliese Michel serves as a reminder of the need for a balanced and compassionate approach to mental health care that respects both scientific understanding and individual beliefs.

In the decades since Anneliese Michel's death, the Catholic Church has revised its guidelines for exorcism, emphasizing the need for thorough medical and psychological evaluation before considering exorcism as an option. The Church now stresses that many symptoms attributed to possession can have natural explanations and that exorcism should be a last resort after all other avenues have been explored.

Despite these changes, the exorcism of Anneliese Michel remains a powerful and cautionary tale about the complexities of human suffering, the limits of medical and spiritual intervention, and the profound impact of cultural and religious beliefs on our understanding of health and illness. The story continues to resonate, provoking reflection on the nature of belief, the power of faith, and the sometimes tragic consequences of our attempts to confront the unknown.

Chapter 6: The Ghosts of the Tower of London

The Tower of London, an iconic fortress and one of the most famous historical landmarks in the world, has a rich and often dark history that spans over a thousand years. Located on the north bank of the River Thames in central London, the Tower has served various roles throughout its existence, including a royal palace, a prison, a treasury, and even a zoo. Its long and storied past has been marked by intrigue, treachery, and violence, contributing to its reputation as one of the most haunted places in the United Kingdom. Tales of ghostly apparitions and supernatural occurrences within its ancient walls have fascinated and terrified visitors for centuries.

The construction of the Tower of London began in 1078 under the orders of William the Conqueror, shortly after his victory at the Battle of Hastings in 1066. The original structure, known as the White Tower, was designed as a symbol of Norman power and dominance over the newly conquered land. Over the centuries, the complex was expanded and fortified, becoming a formidable stronghold and a symbol of royal authority.

One of the most famous ghost stories associated with the Tower of London is that of Anne Boleyn, the second wife of King Henry VIII. Anne Boleyn was arrested and imprisoned in the Tower on charges of adultery, incest, and treason. Despite a lack of credible evidence, she was found guilty and beheaded on Tower Green on May 19, 1536. Anne Boleyn's ghost is said to haunt various parts of the Tower, most notably the chapel of St. Peter ad Vincula, where she is buried. Witnesses have reported seeing her spectral figure walking the corridors, sometimes carrying her severed head. Her presence is often associated with a sense of sadness and unease, reflecting the tragic and unjust nature of her death.

Another well-known ghostly figure is that of Thomas Becket, the Archbishop of Canterbury, who was murdered in Canterbury Cathedral in 1170. According to legend, Becket's ghost appeared at the Tower during the reign of King Henry III to protest the construction of a building on the site of the ancient chapel of St. Peter. His apparition was said to have struck the new building with a cross, causing it to collapse. This story underscores the historical significance of the Tower and its connection to key events and figures in English history.

The Princes in the Tower, Edward V and his younger brother Richard, Duke of York, are also central to the Tower's haunted lore. The young princes were sent to the Tower in 1483 by their uncle, Richard, Duke of Gloucester, who became King Richard III. The boys were declared illegitimate and disappeared under mysterious circumstances, presumed murdered. In 1674, workmen discovered two small skeletons buried under a staircase in the White Tower, which were believed to be the remains of the princes. Their ghosts have been reportedly seen in the Bloody Tower, where they are said to appear holding hands, their faces etched with sorrow and fear.

Lady Jane Grey, known as the "Nine Days' Queen," is another tragic figure whose ghost is said to haunt the Tower of London. Jane Grey was proclaimed queen in July 1553 but was deposed by Mary I less than two weeks later. Imprisoned in the Tower, Jane was eventually executed on February 12, 1554. Her ghost has been sighted in various parts of the Tower, including the battlements and the rooms where she was held captive. Witnesses describe her apparition as a pale, sad figure, reflecting the brief and turbulent nature of her reign and the injustice of her execution.

The Tower's history as a place of imprisonment and execution has contributed to its haunted reputation. During the Tudor period, the Tower became infamous for its role in the political machinations and brutal executions of the time. The story of Margaret Pole, Countess of Salisbury, is particularly harrowing. An ardent Catholic and member of the Plantagenet family, Margaret was imprisoned by Henry VIII and executed in 1541. Her execution was notoriously botched, with the inexperienced executioner requiring several blows to complete the task. Her ghost is said to haunt the site of her execution, often appearing as a wailing, distressed figure.

Another notable ghost is that of Sir Walter Raleigh, an explorer, soldier, and writer who was imprisoned in the Tower multiple times during his tumultuous career. Raleigh spent many years in the Tower, during which he wrote several of his works. He was eventually executed in 1618. His ghost is said to roam the Tower's grounds, particularly near the Bloody Tower where he was held. Raleigh's spirit is often described as contemplative, reflecting his years of imprisonment and intellectual pursuits within the Tower's walls.

In addition to these well-known figures, the Tower of London is said to be haunted by numerous other spirits, including soldiers, prisoners, and even animals. The Tower has a long history as a royal menagerie, housing exotic animals such as lions, bears, and elephants. Ghostly sightings of these animals, particularly lions, have been reported, adding to the eerie atmosphere of the site.

The Tower's Yeoman Warders, commonly known as Beefeaters, have also reported numerous paranormal encounters. These guards, who live within the Tower's walls, have experienced unexplained phenomena such as sudden drops in temperature, disembodied voices, and shadowy figures moving through the corridors. Their accounts lend credibility to the Tower's haunted reputation, as they are intimately familiar with the site and its history.

One of the most chilling ghost stories involves the spectral appearance of a procession of prisoners being led to their executions. Witnesses have described seeing this ghostly parade, complete with guards and a condemned prisoner, moving silently through the Tower grounds. This haunting serves as a poignant reminder of the Tower's grim role as a place of death and punishment.

Despite its haunted reputation, the Tower of London remains a popular tourist destination, attracting millions of visitors each year. Its rich history, architectural grandeur, and storied past make it a fascinating site for those interested in history and the paranormal. The ghost stories associated with the Tower continue to captivate the imagination, adding an element of mystery and intrigue to this historic landmark.

The enduring fascination with the ghosts of the Tower of London can be attributed to the site's deep connection to significant historical events and figures. The tales of spectral appearances and supernatural occurrences provide a unique lens through which to explore the Tower's past, offering a sense of continuity between the present and the distant, often tumultuous, history of England. Whether one believes in ghosts or not, the stories of the Tower's haunted past serve as a powerful testament to the enduring legacy of this iconic fortress and its place in the collective memory of the nation.

Chapter 7: The Curse of the Pharaohs

The Curse of the Pharaohs is one of the most enduring and captivating legends in the realm of archaeology and ancient history. It refers to the alleged curse that is said to befall anyone who disturbs the tombs of the ancient Egyptian pharaohs. This curse is purportedly responsible for a series of misfortunes, illnesses, and deaths that have befallen those who have entered or otherwise disturbed these ancient resting places. The legend gained worldwide fame with the discovery of the tomb of Tutankhamun in 1922 by British archaeologist Howard Carter, but its roots and stories stretch back much further into history.

The concept of the Curse of the Pharaohs is deeply intertwined with the ancient Egyptians' beliefs about the afterlife. The Egyptians believed that death was not the end but rather a transition to a new existence. They prepared extensively for the afterlife, ensuring that the deceased would be well-equipped for eternity. This preparation involved elaborate burial practices, including the construction of tombs filled with treasures, food, clothing, and other items thought necessary for the journey. To protect these tombs from grave robbers and to safeguard the sanctity of the deceased's final resting place, the Egyptians sometimes inscribed curses on the walls of the tombs. These curses were intended to invoke divine protection and to deter any would-be intruders with threats of supernatural retribution.

One of the earliest and most famous examples of such a curse comes from the tomb of Khentika Ikhekhi, a Sixth Dynasty official. The curse reads: "As for all men who shall enter this my tomb impure, there will be judgment... an end shall be made for him... I shall seize his neck like that of a bird... I shall cast the fear of myself into him." Such inscriptions were relatively rare and tended to be more of a deterrent rather than an actual belief that they would be magically enforced.

The modern fascination with the Curse of the Pharaohs began in earnest with the discovery of the tomb of Tutankhamun, often referred to as King Tut. Tutankhamun was a relatively minor pharaoh who ruled during the 18th Dynasty, around 1332–1323 BCE. His tomb, located in the Valley of the Kings, was discovered by Howard Carter and his financial backer, Lord Carnarvon, after years of persistent searching. The tomb was remarkably intact and filled with a wealth of artifacts, providing an unprecedented glimpse into the life and death of an ancient Egyptian pharaoh.

Shortly after the tomb was opened, the first significant death occurred. Lord Carnarvon, who had been present at the opening of the tomb, died in April 1923, just a few months after the discovery. His death was attributed to an infected mosquito bite that led to blood poisoning. This event sparked widespread speculation and sensational headlines about a curse associated with Tutankhamun's tomb. The media of the time eagerly latched onto the story, fueling public imagination with tales of ancient retribution.

The purported curse was further sensationalized by the deaths of several other individuals connected to the tomb's discovery. For example, George Jay Gould, a visitor to the tomb, died of a fever shortly after his visit. Arthur Mace, a member of Carter's excavation team, also died of suspected arsenic poisoning in 1928. The untimely deaths of other individuals, including Richard Bethell, Carter's personal secretary, who died under mysterious circumstances in 1929, and Hugh Evelyn-White, another archaeologist who committed suicide, were all linked in the public's mind to the curse of Tutankhamun.

However, a closer examination of the facts reveals that the curse might be more fiction than fact. Many of the people who were present at the tomb's opening or who worked on the excavation lived long, healthy lives. Howard Carter himself, who was perhaps most directly connected to the discovery, lived until 1939, dying of natural causes at the age of 64. Moreover, statistical analyses of the deaths associated with the tomb suggest that the mortality rate among those who entered the tomb was not significantly higher than that of the general population at the time.

Modern explanations for the alleged curse include psychological and physiological factors. The power of suggestion, combined with the media frenzy surrounding the tomb's discovery, may have contributed to a form of collective hysteria, where individuals attributed normal illnesses and accidents to supernatural causes. Additionally, some researchers have suggested that exposure to ancient molds and bacteria within the sealed tomb could have caused infections and illnesses in those who entered. This theory posits that long-sealed environments may harbor pathogens that modern immune systems are not equipped to handle, leading to real but mundane health problems that were misinterpreted as manifestations of a curse.

Despite the skepticism and scientific explanations, the legend of the Curse of the Pharaohs continues to capture the public's imagination. The allure of the curse is bolstered by the mystique of ancient Egypt itself, a civilization that has fascinated people for centuries with its monumental architecture, enigmatic hieroglyphs, and rich mythology. The combination of historical intrigue, archeological discovery, and supernatural speculation creates a compelling narrative that transcends time and continues to be retold in books, films, and popular culture.

The concept of the curse also taps into broader themes of human curiosity and the boundaries of knowledge. The discovery of Tutankhamun's tomb was a milestone in the field of archaeology, representing the culmination of years of diligent work and the promise of uncovering the secrets of a long-lost world. The notion of a curse serves as a symbolic reminder of the potential dangers and ethical considerations inherent in such endeavors. It raises questions about the respect owed to the dead and the consequences of disturbing their resting places for the sake of scientific or personal gain.

In addition to Tutankhamun, other pharaohs and tombs have been associated with similar legends of curses and supernatural protection. The tombs of the great pyramids of Giza, built for pharaohs Khufu, Khafre, and Menkaure, have also inspired tales of ancient curses. While there is little concrete evidence to support these stories, they contribute to the mystique and fascination surrounding these monumental structures.

The enduring appeal of the Curse of the Pharaohs lies in its blend of historical fact, myth, and mystery. It reflects humanity's fascination with death and the afterlife, as well as our enduring curiosity about the ancient world. Whether viewed as a genuine supernatural phenomenon or a product of cultural imagination, the curse serves as a powerful narrative that continues to captivate and inspire.

Chapter 8: The Brown Lady of Raynham Hall

The Brown Lady of Raynham Hall is one of the most famous and enduring ghost stories in British folklore, known for its eerie presence and the iconic photograph that supposedly captured her spectral form. Raynham Hall, located in Norfolk, England, is a grand country house that has been the seat of the Townshend family for over three centuries. The ghostly figure known as the Brown Lady is said to be the spirit of Lady Dorothy Walpole, the sister of Sir Robert Walpole, Britain's first Prime Minister, and the second wife of Charles Townshend, the 2nd Viscount Townshend.

Lady Dorothy Walpole was born in 1686 and grew up in a prominent aristocratic family. She married Charles Townshend in 1713, becoming the mistress of Raynham Hall. Her marriage, however, was marked by unhappiness and tragedy. It is believed that Dorothy was imprisoned in her room at Raynham Hall by her jealous and vengeful husband, who had discovered her infidelity. According to legend, she was kept in isolation until her death from smallpox in 1726, though some versions of the story suggest she was pushed down the grand staircase by her husband, which led to her death.

The first recorded sighting of the Brown Lady occurred in 1835, during a festive gathering at Raynham Hall. Guests reported seeing a ghostly figure in a brown brocade dress wandering the corridors. The sightings continued sporadically over the years, and many people claimed to have encountered the apparition. The most famous encounter, however, took place on Christmas Eve in 1835 when Colonel Loftus and another guest, Hawkins, saw the Brown Lady on the grand staircase. Loftus described her as an ethereal figure with empty eye sockets and a ghastly visage, dressed in a rich brown satin dress.

In 1836, Captain Frederick Marryat, a friend of the Townshend family and a noted novelist, stayed at Raynham Hall. Skeptical of the ghost stories, he requested to spend the night in the haunted room. Armed with a pistol, he was prepared for any mischief. During his stay, he had a chilling encounter with the Brown Lady. He claimed that the ghost appeared before him, holding a lantern and grinning malevolently. Terrified, Marryat fired his pistol at the apparition, but the bullet passed through her, and she vanished. Marryat later wrote about his experience, adding credibility to the legend of the Brown Lady.

The most compelling evidence of the Brown Lady's existence came in 1936 when Country Life magazine published a photograph taken by Captain Hubert C. Provand and his assistant, Indre Shira. The two photographers were documenting the architecture of Raynham Hall when they captured an image of a spectral figure descending the staircase. The photograph shows a ghostly, translucent figure in a flowing gown, which many believe to be the Brown Lady. This photograph is often cited as one of the most convincing pieces of evidence for the existence of ghosts.

The photograph generated significant interest and debate. Some skeptics suggested that it was the result of double exposure or other photographic trickery, but Provand and Shira maintained that it was genuine. Over the years, the photograph has been analyzed and scrutinized, yet it remains one of the most iconic images in the history of paranormal investigation.

Sightings of the Brown Lady have continued sporadically throughout the 20th and 21st centuries. Many visitors and staff at Raynham Hall have reported strange occurrences, such as unexplained cold spots, the sensation of being watched, and the sound of footsteps in empty corridors. Some have even claimed to have seen the ghostly figure of Lady Dorothy herself, often appearing sad and forlorn.

Several theories have been proposed to explain the phenomenon of the Brown Lady. One theory is that the ghost is a residual haunting, a type of haunting in which a traumatic event from the past is replayed repeatedly, like a recording. In this case, the traumatic event could be Lady Dorothy's imprisonment and subsequent death. Residual hauntings are often thought to be imprints of energy left behind by intense emotions or significant events.

Another theory is that the Brown Lady is an intelligent haunting, meaning that the spirit is aware of its surroundings and can interact with the living. This theory is supported by the numerous accounts of the Brown Lady's interactions with witnesses, such as Captain Marryat's encounter and the photograph taken by Provand and Shira. Proponents of this theory believe that Lady Dorothy's spirit remains at Raynham Hall due to unresolved issues or a desire to protect her former home.

Skeptics, however, argue that the sightings and experiences can be explained by psychological and environmental factors. They suggest that the legend of the Brown Lady has created a powerful expectation of encountering a ghost, leading to misinterpretations of natural phenomena or the power of suggestion. For example, the eerie atmosphere of an old mansion, combined with stories of ghosts, could cause people to perceive normal sounds and shadows as paranormal activity.

Despite the skepticism, the story of the Brown Lady of Raynham Hall remains a compelling and enduring legend. The combination of historical intrigue, personal tragedy, and supernatural mystery has captured the imagination of countless people. The photograph of the Brown Lady continues to be one of the most famous and debated images in the annals of ghost lore, and Raynham Hall remains a site of fascination for paranormal enthusiasts and historians alike.

The legend of the Brown Lady also highlights broader themes in the study of hauntings and ghost stories. It reflects the human fascination with the unknown and the afterlife, as well as the ways in which personal and collective memories can shape our perceptions of the past. Ghost stories like that of the Brown Lady serve as cultural touchstones, connecting us to history and to the enduring mysteries that lie beyond the veil of death.

In recent years, the story of the Brown Lady has inspired numerous books, documentaries, and television programs, further cementing its place in popular culture. Paranormal investigators continue to visit Raynham Hall, hoping to catch a glimpse of the elusive specter or to uncover new evidence of her existence. While the mystery of the Brown Lady may never be fully resolved, her story continues to captivate and intrigue those who seek to understand the supernatural.

Chapter 9: The Winchester Mystery House

The Winchester Mystery House, located in San Jose, California, is one of the most enigmatic and fascinating architectural marvels in the United States. This sprawling, eccentric mansion, which covers 24,000 square feet, is renowned not only for its size and grandeur but also for its bizarre and labyrinthine design. The house was the creation of Sarah Winchester, the widow of William Wirt Winchester, heir to the Winchester Repeating Arms Company fortune. The mansion's history, combined with its architectural oddities and the mysterious life of its owner, has led to numerous legends and theories, making it a magnet for ghost hunters, historians, and curiosity seekers alike.

Sarah Lockwood Pardee Winchester was born in 1839 in New Haven, Connecticut. She married William Wirt Winchester in 1862, and the couple led a privileged life thanks to the enormous profits generated by the Winchester rifle, a revolutionary firearm that played a significant role in the American Civil War and the subsequent expansion of the American frontier. However, Sarah's life was marred by tragedy. In 1866, she and William lost their only child, Annie, to a rare childhood illness. This devastating loss was compounded when William died of tuberculosis in 1881, leaving Sarah a wealthy but grief-stricken widow.

Overwhelmed by grief and seeking solace, Sarah turned to spiritualism, a popular movement in the late 19th century that professed communication with the dead. According to legend, a Boston medium told Sarah that her family was cursed by the spirits of those killed by the Winchester rifle. The medium allegedly advised her to move west and build a house for these restless spirits to appease them. The only catch was that construction on the house should never cease, as continuous building would keep the spirits at bay and prevent further misfortune.

In 1884, Sarah Winchester purchased an unfinished farmhouse in the Santa Clara Valley and began what would become an epic building project that lasted 38 years, until her death in 1922. She employed teams of carpenters, masons, and craftsmen who worked around the clock, seven days a week, to expand and remodel the house. The result was a sprawling, seven-story mansion with 160 rooms, including 40 bedrooms, two ballrooms, 47 fireplaces, 17 chimneys, over 10,000 panes of glass, two basements, three elevators, and a multitude of staircases, doors, and hallways that seem to lead nowhere.

The design of the Winchester Mystery House is a testament to Sarah's eccentricity and the purported spiritual guidance she received. The mansion is filled with architectural oddities and anomalies that defy conventional logic and design principles. There are doors that open onto blank walls, staircases that ascend to ceilings, windows that overlook other rooms, and hallways that twist and turn unpredictably. Some believe that these perplexing features were intended to confuse and thwart the malevolent spirits Sarah feared, creating a maze-like environment that would trap or mislead them.

One of the most famous features of the house is the "Staircase to Nowhere," a set of stairs that ascends several flights only to end abruptly at the ceiling. Similarly, there is the "Door to Nowhere," which opens to a sheer drop outside the building. These peculiar elements have sparked countless theories and speculations. Some suggest that Sarah's irrational design choices were the result of her deteriorating mental state, while others believe they were deliberate attempts to create a labyrinth that would protect her from vengeful spirits.

In addition to its architectural strangeness, the Winchester Mystery House was also equipped with many innovative features for its time. Sarah was deeply interested in modern technology and ensured that her mansion was outfitted with the latest conveniences. The house boasts indoor plumbing, hot water, forced-air heating, and push-button gas lights. It even had one of the first working elevators on the West Coast. These modern amenities reflect Sarah's wealth and her desire to create a comfortable, albeit peculiar, living environment.

Despite its grandeur and modernity, the mansion was never completed. Construction halted abruptly upon Sarah Winchester's death in 1922, leaving many rooms unfinished and numerous projects abandoned. Sarah's will, which she drafted in a unique, handwritten code, revealed her deep paranoia and obsession with secrecy. She left her vast fortune to various charities, her favorite niece, and her loyal staff, but made no specific provisions for the mansion itself. Consequently, the house was auctioned off and eventually became a tourist attraction, drawing visitors eager to explore its mysteries and hear its ghostly tales.

The Winchester Mystery House is reputed to be haunted by the spirits of those killed by the Winchester rifle, as well as by Sarah Winchester herself. Over the years, numerous visitors and employees have reported strange occurrences and supernatural phenomena within its walls. Some claim to have seen ghostly apparitions, including a spectral figure believed to be Sarah, wandering the halls and overseeing the ongoing construction. Others have reported hearing unexplained footsteps, voices, and the sound of hammering, as if the construction crews of old are still at work.

In addition to these ghostly sightings, many have experienced physical sensations such as sudden cold spots, the feeling of being watched, and unexplained touches. These experiences have led paranormal investigators and ghost hunters to flock to the mansion, hoping to capture evidence of the supernatural. The house has been featured on numerous television programs, including "Ghost Adventures," "Most Haunted," and "Scariest Places on Earth," further cementing its reputation as one of America's most haunted locations.

Theories about the true nature of the Winchester Mystery House abound. Some suggest that Sarah Winchester was not driven by fear of spirits but was instead a creative genius who used her immense wealth to indulge her architectural whims. Others believe that she may have been suffering from a psychological disorder, such as obsessive-compulsive disorder or schizophrenia, which manifested in her compulsive building and erratic design choices. Regardless of the true motivation behind the mansion's construction, there is no denying its unique place in American history and its enduring allure.

The Winchester Mystery House stands as a testament to the power of grief, guilt, and the human desire to find meaning and solace in the face of tragedy. It is a physical embodiment of one woman's attempt to come to terms with her losses and the perceived consequences of her family's legacy. The house's intricate design, filled with dead ends and secret passages, mirrors the labyrinthine nature of the human mind, where the line between reality and imagination can often blur.

Chapter 10: The Dyatlov Pass Incident

The Dyatlov Pass Incident remains one of the most perplexing and enduring mysteries in modern history. Occurring in 1959 in the Ural Mountains of the Soviet Union, this event involved the unexplained deaths of nine experienced hikers from the Ural Polytechnical Institute. The group, led by Igor Dyatlov, embarked on a journey intended to reach Otorten, a mountain north of their starting point. However, what was meant to be a challenging but straightforward expedition turned into a nightmare, leading to a series of events that has baffled investigators, researchers, and conspiracy theorists for decades.

The group set out on January 27, 1959, with high spirits and meticulous preparation. They established their camp on the slopes of Kholat Syakhl, which translates to "Dead Mountain" in the local Mansi language, on February 1. On this fateful night, something catastrophic happened that drove the hikers out of their tent into the harsh, sub-zero temperatures. When the search and rescue team found the hikers' tent on February 26, it had been cut open from the inside, suggesting that the occupants fled in a state of panic. The discovery of the bodies raised more questions than answers.

Initially, the bodies of Yuri Doroshenko, Lyudmila Dubinina, Alexander Kolevatov, Zinaida Kolmogorova, Rustem Slobodin, and Igor Dyatlov himself were found at various locations around the campsite. The hikers were inadequately dressed, wearing only socks or a single shoe, despite the severe cold. This detail alone suggested that whatever had frightened them was more terrifying than the prospect of freezing to death. Doroshenko and Krivonischenko were found near a makeshift fire under a cedar tree, with branches broken up to five meters high, indicating they had climbed the tree, perhaps in an attempt to spot something or someone. The bodies of Dyatlov, Kolmogorova, and Slobodin were found in a line, indicating they had been trying to return to the tent. Slobodin's skull had a minor fracture, but it was not deemed fatal.

Two months later, the remaining four hikers were found in a ravine 75 meters further into the woods. These bodies provided even more unsettling clues. Nicolas Thibeaux-Brignollel had suffered significant skull damage. Lyudmila Dubinina and Alexander Kolevatov had severe chest fractures, which forensic experts compared to the force of a car crash. Dubinina was also missing her tongue, eyes, part of the lips, as well as facial tissue and a fragment of skull bone. Adding to the bizarre circumstances, some of the clothing recovered from the bodies was found to be radioactive.

The official Soviet investigation concluded that the group members had died due to a "compelling natural force," but this vague statement did little to quell speculation. Over the years, numerous theories have been proposed to explain the Dyatlov Pass Incident. Some suggest an avalanche forced the hikers to flee in panic. However, the slope on which they camped was not steep enough to trigger an avalanche, and the physical injuries sustained by the hikers did not align with those typically caused by such an event. Moreover, the experienced hikers would have known how to react in such a situation.

Other theories propose a military involvement, suggesting that the group might have inadvertently stumbled upon a secret military testing site and been caught in the crossfire or exposed to a weapon test. This idea is supported by reports of strange orange orbs seen in the sky around the time of the incident, possibly indicating military aircraft or missile tests. The presence of radioactive clothing also adds weight to this theory, although the source of the radiation has never been conclusively identified.

Some researchers have speculated about a possible encounter with a yeti or other unknown creature, driven by the severe physical trauma and the terror that drove the hikers from their tent. This theory, while popular among enthusiasts of the paranormal, lacks substantial evidence. Similarly, infrasound-induced panic has been suggested, where specific wind patterns could produce sound waves that cause irrational fear and physical discomfort. While plausible, this theory does not fully account for the extent of the injuries.

The Mansi people, indigenous to the region, were also briefly considered suspects. However, there was no evidence of another human presence on the mountain apart from the hikers, and the Mansi were generally known to be peaceful and had no motive to harm the group.

The Dyatlov Pass Incident has also been linked to more outlandish theories, including alien abduction or involvement. Proponents of this idea cite the unexplained lights in the sky and the absence of other plausible explanations. Yet, as with many paranormal theories, this lacks empirical support.

Despite the passage of time and numerous investigations, including a 2019 Russian inquiry that revisited the case and attributed the deaths to a combination of an avalanche and hypothermia, the mystery of the Dyatlov Pass Incident endures. The case is marked by its disturbing details, such as the state of undress, the significant injuries, the strange behavior that led them to abandon their tent, and the radioactivity. Each piece of evidence seems to contradict another, creating a puzzle that may never be fully solved.

What keeps the Dyatlov Pass Incident in the public eye is not just the gruesome fate of the nine hikers but the sheer number of unanswered questions it raises. It remains a cautionary tale about the power and unpredictability of nature, the potential hidden dangers within remote landscapes, and the limits of human understanding when faced with the unknown. This case continues to captivate and intrigue, representing the quintessential unsolved mystery where every theory, no matter how outlandish, seems to hold a kernel of truth, and every answer only leads to more questions.

Chapter 11: The Bermuda Triangle Disappearances

The Bermuda Triangle, also known as the Devil's Triangle, is a loosely defined region in the western part of the North Atlantic Ocean, where numerous aircraft and ships have disappeared under mysterious circumstances. The area is bounded by points in Miami, Bermuda, and Puerto Rico, forming a triangle roughly 500,000 square miles in size. Despite its fame, the Bermuda Triangle is not officially recognized by the U.S. Board on Geographic Names, and there is no universally agreed-upon boundary for the region. The legend of the Bermuda Triangle began to take shape in the early 20th century and has since become one of the most enduring and controversial paranormal phenomena.

The Bermuda Triangle first gained public attention in 1950 when Edward Van Winkle Jones wrote an article in the Miami Herald about the disappearance of ships and planes in the region. Two years later, Fate magazine published an article by George X. Sand, detailing the loss of Flight 19, a group of five U.S. Navy bombers on a training mission. Flight 19 took off from Fort Lauderdale, Florida, on December 5, 1945, and soon encountered navigational difficulties. The squadron leader, Lieutenant Charles Taylor, reported that his compasses were malfunctioning and that he was unsure of their position. Despite efforts to guide them back to base, radio contact was lost, and the planes were never seen again. Adding to the mystery, a Martin PBM Mariner flying boat sent to search for the missing aircraft also vanished with 13 crew members on board.

The disappearances in the Bermuda Triangle have been attributed to various causes, ranging from natural explanations to the supernatural. One of the most commonly cited natural explanations is the region's unique weather patterns. The Bermuda Triangle is prone to sudden and severe storms, which can create dangerous conditions for ships and aircraft. Waterspouts, which are tornadoes that occur over the sea, are also frequent in the area and can be deadly for smaller vessels. Additionally, the Gulf Stream, a strong ocean current that flows through the Triangle, can quickly erase any evidence of a disaster, making it difficult to find wreckage.

Another natural explanation involves underwater topography. The seafloor in the Bermuda Triangle is characterized by deep ocean trenches and underwater mountains. These features can create navigational hazards and contribute to the rapid sinking of ships. The area is also known for methane hydrate deposits, which, when released, can reduce the density of the water and cause ships to sink. Methane gas can also rise to the surface and potentially interfere with the instruments of aircraft, leading to crashes.

Despite these plausible natural explanations, the Bermuda Triangle has also been the subject of numerous supernatural and extraterrestrial theories. One popular theory suggests that the Triangle is a gateway to another dimension or a time portal. Proponents of this idea point to the sudden and unexplained disappearances of ships and planes, suggesting that they may have been transported to another realm. Another theory involves the lost city of Atlantis, with some believing that advanced technology from the ancient civilization could be responsible for the strange occurrences in the area.

Extraterrestrial involvement has also been proposed as an explanation for the Bermuda Triangle disappearances. Some believe that UFOs are responsible for abducting ships and planes, with the Triangle serving as a hotspot for alien activity. This theory gained popularity in the 1960s and 1970s, coinciding with the rise of UFO sightings and interest in extraterrestrial life. While there is no concrete evidence to support these claims, they continue to capture the imagination of many.

In addition to natural and supernatural explanations, human error and equipment failure have played significant roles in many Bermuda Triangle incidents. Inexperienced pilots and navigators, mechanical failures, and miscommunication have all contributed to accidents in the region. For example, Flight 19's disappearance can be partly attributed to Lieutenant Taylor's navigational errors and the squadron's failure to follow standard procedures. Similarly, the loss of the USS Cyclops in 1918, one of the most famous Bermuda Triangle disappearances, was likely due to a combination of overloading, structural issues, and bad weather.

The Bermuda Triangle has also been linked to numerous myths and legends. One of the most enduring is the story of the Mary Celeste, a ship found adrift and deserted in the Atlantic Ocean in 1872. While the Mary Celeste was not found within the Bermuda Triangle, its mysterious abandonment has often been associated with the region's lore. The crew of the Mary Celeste was never found, and the ship's cargo was intact, leading to speculation about what could have caused the crew to abandon ship.

Another famous incident is the disappearance of the SS Marine Sulphur Queen, a tanker carrying molten sulfur that vanished in 1963. Despite extensive search efforts, no trace of the ship or its crew was ever found. The ship's disappearance has been attributed to various causes, including an explosion, structural failure, or foul play. However, the lack of evidence has fueled speculation and contributed to the mystique of the Bermuda Triangle.

Skeptics argue that the number of disappearances in the Bermuda Triangle is not significantly higher than in any other heavily traveled region of the world. They point out that the area is one of the busiest shipping lanes and air traffic corridors, with thousands of vessels and aircraft passing through it each year. Given the high volume of traffic, it is not surprising that accidents occur. Additionally, advancements in navigation and communication technology have reduced the number of incidents in recent years, suggesting that many of the earlier disappearances could be attributed to outdated equipment and techniques.

Despite these arguments, the Bermuda Triangle continues to be a subject of fascination and debate. Numerous books, documentaries, and films have explored the mystery, often emphasizing the more sensational aspects of the phenomenon. The Bermuda Triangle has become a cultural icon, representing the unknown and the unexplained. It serves as a reminder of the ocean's vastness and the potential dangers that lie beneath its surface.

In recent years, scientific research has provided more insights into the natural phenomena that could explain the Bermuda Triangle disappearances. Studies of underwater topography, ocean currents, and weather patterns have shed light on the conditions that can lead to accidents in the region. Advances in technology, such as satellite imagery and deep-sea exploration, have also improved our understanding of the Triangle's mysteries. However, despite these advancements, the Bermuda Triangle retains its allure as a place of intrigue and wonder.

The legacy of the Bermuda Triangle is one of enduring mystery and fascination. It challenges our understanding of the natural world and our desire to find explanations for the inexplicable. Whether viewed as a region plagued by natural hazards, a site of supernatural activity, or a combination of both, the Bermuda Triangle continues to captivate the imagination. Its story is a testament to the power of the unknown and the human drive to explore and uncover the secrets of our world.

Chapter 12: The Ghost Ship SS Ourang Medan

The story of the SS Ourang Medan is one of the most chilling and enigmatic maritime mysteries ever recorded. The tale begins in the late 1940s with a series of distress signals reportedly received by nearby ships navigating the waters of the Strait of Malacca, a busy shipping route between the Malay Peninsula and the Indonesian island of Sumatra. The distress calls came from the Dutch freighter SS Ourang Medan. The messages were received in Morse code and were highly fragmented and incoherent. One of the most alarming transmissions was a short, haunting message: "All officers, including captain, are dead. Lying in chartroom and bridge. Possibly whole crew dead." This was followed by a final, chilling Morse code message: "I die."

The closest ship to respond to the distress signal was the American merchant vessel, the SS Silver Star. The ship promptly altered its course and headed towards the coordinates provided by the Ourang Medan's distress calls. When the Silver Star arrived at the location, they found the Ourang Medan adrift, with no visible signs of damage to its structure. The crew of the Silver Star attempted to hail the ship, but there was no response. A boarding party was assembled to investigate the silent and foreboding vessel.

As the crew of the Silver Star boarded the Ourang Medan, they were met with a sight that would remain seared in their memories. The deck was strewn with the bodies of the Dutch freighter's crew, all apparently frozen in various states of terror and agony. Their eyes were wide open, mouths agape as if trying to scream, and their arms stretched out as if fending off some unseen assailant. The scene below deck was equally grim, with more bodies found in similar conditions, and the ship's dog was found dead, mid-growl at some unknown threat.

The condition of the bodies suggested that the crew had died suddenly and mysteriously. There were no signs of physical trauma, violence, or struggle. The temperature on the ship was unnaturally cold, even though the weather was warm and tropical. The Silver Star's crew noticed an eerie, almost otherworldly silence permeating the vessel. Even more unsettling was the complete lack of any clear indication of what had caused the mass fatalities. The ship's cargo hold was examined but revealed nothing out of the ordinary, further deepening the mystery.

As the boarding party explored the ship, they quickly realized that staying on board posed significant risks. The unnaturally cold air and the growing sense of dread prompted the captain of the Silver Star to make a swift decision to tow the Ourang Medan to the nearest port for a thorough investigation. However, as they prepared to do so, smoke began to billow from the lower decks of the Ourang Medan. The boarding party barely had time to return to their ship before the Ourang Medan was rocked by a massive explosion, which ripped through the hull and sank the ship almost immediately. The cause of the explosion was never determined, but it ensured that the ghostly vessel and its secrets were lost to the depths of the ocean.

The story of the SS Ourang Medan has since become a legend in maritime lore, often cited as one of the most baffling ghost ship tales. Over the years, numerous theories have been proposed to explain the mysterious deaths of the crew. One of the more plausible theories suggests that the ship may have been carrying a hazardous cargo, possibly a combination of potassium cyanide and nitroglycerin. These chemicals, if not properly stored, could produce lethal fumes and cause a sudden toxic reaction, leading to the swift and agonizing deaths of the crew. The explosion could have been triggered by the volatile nature of the cargo, causing the ship to sink before any further investigation could take place.

Another theory speculates that the Ourang Medan may have been involved in some covert military operation or was transporting biological weapons or nerve agents. The sudden and unexplained deaths, along with the apparent lack of physical injuries, could point to exposure to a deadly substance. This theory is bolstered by the Cold War context of the time, where secretive and dangerous cargo was not uncommon.

There are also those who believe that the Ourang Medan's fate was the result of paranormal or extraterrestrial intervention. The eerie conditions on board, the frozen expressions of terror on the faces of the crew, and the unexplained coldness have led some to speculate about encounters with otherworldly forces. These theories, while lacking in concrete evidence, continue to capture the imagination of those who are drawn to the mysterious and unexplained.

Skeptics argue that the tale of the SS Ourang Medan may be nothing more than an elaborate maritime legend or a case of mistaken identity. They point to the lack of official records of a ship by that name, the absence of corroborating evidence, and the dubious origins of the initial reports. Some suggest that the story was fabricated or exaggerated over time, becoming a part of seafaring folklore.

Despite the skepticism, the story of the SS Ourang Medan persists, largely because of the chilling nature of the reported events and the compelling mystery at its core. It serves as a reminder of the many dangers that lurk at sea and the numerous unexplained phenomena that continue to baffle and intrigue us. The ocean, with its vastness and unpredictability, has always been a source of both wonder and fear. The tale of the Ourang Medan fits neatly into this narrative, highlighting the thin line between the known and the unknown.

Further complicating efforts to uncover the truth are the inconsistencies and gaps in the historical record. Accounts of the Ourang Medan vary, with some details differing significantly depending on the source. These discrepancies make it difficult to separate fact from fiction and add another layer of mystery to the story. The lack of physical evidence, due to the ship's destruction, means that much of what is known is based on anecdotal reports and second-hand accounts, which can often be unreliable or exaggerated.

In recent years, modern researchers and maritime historians have attempted to piece together the puzzle using available data and historical context. Some have looked into shipping records, naval logs, and other archival materials to find any reference to the Ourang Medan or similar incidents. While these efforts have yet to provide a definitive answer, they have contributed to a better understanding of the period and the possible explanations for the events described.

The ghost ship SS Ourang Medan remains one of the sea's greatest enigmas, a haunting tale that continues to capture the imagination of those who hear it. Whether viewed as a cautionary tale about the dangers of hazardous cargo, a story of secret military operations gone awry, or a glimpse into the paranormal, the mystery of the Ourang Medan endures. It stands as a testament to the enduring power of maritime legends and the human fascination with the unknown. The truth, buried somewhere in the depths of the ocean, may never be fully uncovered, but the story will undoubtedly continue to be told and retold, captivating new generations of adventurers and mystery seekers.

Chapter 13: The Black Monk of Pontefract

The Black Monk of Pontefract is considered one of the most violent and well-documented hauntings in British history. The haunting took place in a modest semi-detached house at 30 East Drive, on the Chequerfields Estate in Pontefract, West Yorkshire. The events began in the late 1960s and centered around the Pritchard family, who had moved into the house in August 1966. The family consisted of Jean and Joe Pritchard, their son Philip, and their daughter Diane. Over the years, the house gained notoriety as a hotbed of supernatural activity, and the entity responsible for the disturbances came to be known as the Black Monk, purportedly due to the ghostly appearance resembling a monk in black robes.

The haunting began with relatively minor incidents, which the Pritchards initially dismissed as harmless pranks or the result of natural causes. The first event occurred when Philip, aged 15, and his grandmother were alone in the house. A strange cold gust of wind swept through the house, despite it being a warm August day. Moments later, white powder-like substance began falling from the ceiling, which could not be traced to any obvious source. The family cleaned up the powder, but it continued to reappear, accompanied by puddles of water that would form and disappear mysteriously.

As the days passed, the activity escalated. Lights would turn on and off by themselves, objects would move or levitate, and furniture would be overturned. One particularly frightening incident involved the family's tea dispenser, which began operating on its own, flinging hot tea around the kitchen. Heavy furniture, such as chests of drawers and wardrobes, would move across the floor of their own accord, and strange noises, including loud bangs and the sound of footsteps, would echo throughout the house.

The disturbances seemed to focus particularly on the Pritchards' teenage daughter, Diane. She experienced the most direct and terrifying encounters with the entity. On several occasions, she was reportedly dragged from her bed by unseen hands, and on one occasion, she was pulled up the stairs by her throat, leaving visible finger marks on her skin. Diane's experiences were particularly traumatic and suggested that the entity had a particular animosity towards her.

The entity was eventually named the Black Monk due to several sightings of a figure in a black robe within the house. The figure was described as having a hood covering its face, giving it a sinister and menacing appearance. The legend behind the Black Monk suggests that he was a 16th-century monk from a nearby priory who had been executed for the rape and murder of a young girl. He was reportedly hanged on the gallows that once stood on the site where the Pritchard's house was built. This gruesome backstory added a chilling dimension to the haunting, suggesting that the malevolent spirit was exacting some form of revenge or retribution.

The Pritchard family sought help from various sources to rid their home of the haunting. They invited local priests to perform exorcisms, but these attempts seemed only to aggravate the spirit, leading to even more intense activity. Paranormal investigators were also brought in, but they, too, could not provide a solution to the haunting. Some investigators managed to capture photographic evidence of orbs and other anomalies, adding to the credibility of the Pritchards' claims. The activity was so severe and relentless that the Pritchard family considered moving out, but they ultimately decided to stay and endure the disturbances.

In addition to the Pritchard family's personal experiences, the house at 30 East Drive became a focal point for paranormal enthusiasts and researchers. Numerous investigations have been conducted over the years, with many investigators reporting unusual phenomena, including unexplained temperature drops, strange noises, and sightings of the Black Monk. Some investigators claimed to have experienced physical attacks, similar to those endured by Diane. The house's reputation grew, attracting media attention and becoming a subject of interest for paranormal documentaries and television shows.

Despite the passage of time, the haunting at 30 East Drive has not been conclusively explained. Skeptics have proposed various natural explanations, such as the effects of electromagnetic fields or psychological factors, but these theories have not satisfactorily accounted for the sheer intensity and variety of the phenomena reported. The case of the Black Monk of Pontefract remains one of the most compelling and puzzling examples of a haunting, notable for its violent and sustained nature.

One of the reasons the Black Monk case is so enduring is the detailed and consistent testimony from the Pritchard family and other witnesses. Over the years, their accounts have been corroborated by independent investigators, neighbors, and even casual visitors to the house, lending a degree of credibility to their claims. The detailed descriptions of the phenomena, combined with the physical evidence and the psychological impact on the family, make it difficult to dismiss the case as mere fabrication or hysteria.

The house at 30 East Drive continues to attract attention to this day, with paranormal investigators and thrill-seekers hoping to experience the supernatural activity firsthand. It has been featured in numerous books, documentaries, and paranormal investigation shows, cementing its place in the annals of paranormal history. The Black Monk of Pontefract has also inspired fictional accounts and dramatizations, further perpetuating the legend.

In analyzing the Black Monk of Pontefract case, it is essential to consider the broader context of poltergeist phenomena and hauntings. The activity described by the Pritchards shares similarities with other well-documented poltergeist cases, such as the Enfield Poltergeist in

London. These cases often involve a combination of physical disturbances, such as objects moving and strange noises, along with apparitions and direct attacks on individuals. Theories about the nature of poltergeists vary, with some researchers suggesting they are manifestations of repressed human emotions or energy, while others believe they are the actions of malevolent spirits or entities.

The Black Monk case also raises questions about the relationship between place and haunting. The historical background of the site, with its connection to a violent and traumatic past, suggests that the location itself may play a significant role in the phenomena. This aligns with the theory that certain places can retain a form of residual energy or imprint from past events, which can manifest as hauntings. The combination of a violent historical event and the construction of the house on the site may have created the conditions for the Black Monk's malevolent presence.

Despite the various theories and investigations, the true nature of the Black Monk of Pontefract remains elusive. The case serves as a reminder of the complexities and mysteries of paranormal phenomena, which often defy simple explanations. It highlights the challenges faced by researchers and investigators in trying to understand and document such events, and the importance of maintaining an open yet critical approach to the study of the paranormal.

The legacy of the Black Monk of Pontefract is one of fear, fascination, and enduring mystery. For the Pritchard family, the haunting was a life-changing and traumatic experience that left a lasting impact. For the wider world, it remains a compelling example of the unexplained, a case that continues to intrigue and baffle those who hear about it. The story of the Black Monk, with its blend of historical tragedy, violent hauntings, and detailed witness accounts, stands as a powerful testament to the enduring power of the supernatural in our collective imagination.

Chapter 14: The Greenbrier Ghost

The Greenbrier Ghost is a fascinating and singular case in the annals of American folklore and legal history. It is unique because it is one of the rare instances where the testimony of a ghost was used to convict a murderer in a court of law. The tale revolves around the mysterious death of Zona Heaster Shue, a young woman from Greenbrier County, West Virginia, whose spectral appearance supposedly revealed the truth about her demise. This eerie narrative is intertwined with themes of love, betrayal, and justice from beyond the grave, making it one of the most intriguing ghost stories in American history.

The story begins with the life and tragic death of Elva Zona Heaster. Born in 1873, Zona was described as a vivacious and attractive young woman. In 1896, she met and quickly married Erasmus (Edward) Stribbling Trout Shue, a drifter who had recently moved to Greenbrier County. Edward, who was known as Trout, worked as a blacksmith and appeared to be a charming and industrious individual. However, he had a checkered past, which was not well-known to the people of Greenbrier. Trout had been married twice before; his first wife had left him due to his violent behavior, and his second wife had died under mysterious circumstances. Despite these red flags, Zona and Trout were married, and Zona's mother, Mary Jane Heaster, was not pleased with the union.

On January 23, 1897, only a few months into their marriage, Zona was found dead in her home. The discovery was made by a young boy sent by Trout on an errand. The boy found Zona lying at the foot of the stairs, stretched out with her legs together, one arm at her side, and the other across her chest. Her head was slightly tilted. Trout was called immediately and, upon arriving, he displayed an unusual amount of emotion, cradling Zona's head and weeping. Dr. George W. Knapp, the local physician and coroner, was summoned, but Trout had already dressed Zona's body in a high-necked, stiff-collared dress and placed a veil over her face. This was unusual, as it was customary for the women of the community to wash and prepare the body. Dr. Knapp's examination was cursory, due to Trout's continuous interference and visible grief, and he concluded that Zona had died of "everlasting faint," later changed to complications from childbirth, despite there being no evidence she was pregnant.

Zona was quickly buried, but her mother, Mary Jane Heaster, was convinced that Trout had something to do with her daughter's death. Mary Jane prayed every night for Zona to return and reveal the truth about her demise. According to Mary Jane, her prayers were answered when Zona's ghost visited her over the course of four nights. The apparition provided a detailed account of how Trout had murdered her. Zona's ghost claimed that Trout had attacked her in a fit of rage because he believed she had not prepared any meat for dinner. He broke her neck, which she demonstrated to her mother by turning her head completely around.

Mary Jane took this information to the local prosecutor, John Alfred Preston, who was initially skeptical but agreed to reopen the case. Dr. Knapp was persuaded to exhume Zona's body for a proper autopsy, which was conducted on February 22, 1897. The examination revealed that Zona's neck had indeed been broken, and her windpipe was crushed. There were finger marks on her neck indicating that she had been strangled. Trout Shue was arrested and charged with the murder of his wife.

The trial of Edward Shue began in June 1897. The prosecution's case was largely circumstantial, but they had the crucial testimony of Dr. Knapp, who confirmed the findings of the autopsy. However, the defense sought to discredit Mary Jane Heaster by focusing on her belief in the ghostly visitation. They argued that she had influenced the reopening of the case due to her superstitions. This strategy backfired when Mary Jane Heaster took the stand. She recounted the story of Zona's ghost visiting her in a calm and detailed manner, and her testimony was so compelling that it had a profound impact on the jury and courtroom observers.

The jury deliberated for just over an hour before returning a verdict of guilty. Edward Shue was sentenced to life in prison. He was spared the death penalty due to the jury's recommendation for mercy, possibly influenced by the unusual nature of the case. Trout was imprisoned in the West Virginia State Penitentiary in Moundsville, where he died three years later in March 1900, the victim of an epidemic. He maintained his innocence to the end.

The story of the Greenbrier Ghost is not just a ghost story; it is a significant case in legal history. It illustrates how folklore and the belief in the supernatural can intersect with the judicial process. The case remains unique because it is one of the few instances where ghostly testimony was apparently instrumental in securing a conviction. Mary Jane Heaster's unwavering belief in her daughter's spectral visitation and her determination to seek justice highlight the powerful role that personal convictions and cultural beliefs can play in legal proceedings.

The Greenbrier Ghost case also provides insight into the social and cultural context of the time. In the late 19th century, rural communities in America were steeped in superstitions and a belief in the supernatural. Stories of ghosts and hauntings were part of the cultural fabric, and people often turned to these beliefs to explain the unexplainable. Mary Jane Heaster's account of her daughter's ghost was not dismissed outright by the community or the legal system, indicating the prevalence and acceptance of such beliefs.

Today, the story of the Greenbrier Ghost continues to captivate the imagination. The house where Zona lived and died is now a private residence, but it attracts attention from those interested in paranormal phenomena and historical curiosities. The tale has been the subject of books, documentaries, and countless retellings, cementing its place in American folklore.

In examining the legacy of the Greenbrier Ghost, it is essential to recognize the elements that make it enduring. The story combines the mystery of an unsolved crime, the emotional appeal of a mother's love and quest for justice, and the eerie intrigue of a ghostly visitation. It touches on universal themes of betrayal, love, and the desire for truth, all wrapped in the chilling cloak of the supernatural.

Moreover, the Greenbrier Ghost case serves as a reminder of the human capacity to seek answers and justice, even in the face of disbelief and ridicule. Mary Jane Heaster's determination to uncover the truth about her daughter's death, despite the initial skepticism she faced, highlights the enduring power of maternal love and the pursuit of justice. Her story is a testament to the belief that the truth, no matter how it is revealed, must be brought to light.

The Greenbrier Ghost is not just a story about a ghost and a murder; it is a story about the human spirit and the lengths to which one will go to find closure and justice. It underscores the interplay between belief and evidence, between folklore and fact, and between the natural and the supernatural. As such, it remains a poignant and compelling narrative that continues to resonate with people today, more than a century after the events took place.

Chapter 15: The Borley Rectory Hauntings

The Borley Rectory hauntings stand out as one of the most notorious and controversial cases of paranormal activity in England. Often referred to as "the most haunted house in England," Borley Rectory was a Victorian mansion located in the village of Borley, Essex. The rectory gained its infamous reputation due to a series of unexplained phenomena reported by its residents and investigators, including ghostly apparitions, mysterious writings on walls, and other poltergeist activities. The saga of Borley Rectory encompasses a mix of historical intrigue, personal tragedies, and the fervent investigations of one of the most famous ghost hunters of the 20th century, Harry Price.

Borley Rectory was constructed in 1862 by Reverend Henry Dawson Ellis Bull. The Bull family lived there for several decades, during which the first accounts of supernatural occurrences began. According to reports, the Bull children claimed to have seen ghostly figures, including a spectral nun who wandered the grounds and a phantom coach driven by headless horsemen. These sightings laid the groundwork for Borley's reputation as a haunted location.

The legend of the spectral nun became one of the most enduring elements of the Borley haunting. According to local lore, the rectory was built on the site of a 13th-century monastery, where a monk and a nun from a nearby nunnery had a forbidden love affair. When their relationship was discovered, the monk was executed, and the nun was bricked up alive within the convent walls. It was said that her restless spirit haunted the rectory grounds, forever searching for her lost love.

The supernatural activity at Borley Rectory gained widespread attention in the late 1920s when Reverend Guy Eric Smith and his wife moved into the rectory. Shortly after their arrival, the Smiths began experiencing a series of inexplicable events. Mrs. Smith reported finding a brown paper package containing a human skull in a cupboard. They also heard unexplained footsteps, experienced objects moving on their own, and witnessed the appearance of mysterious writings on the walls. These events prompted them to contact the Daily Mirror, hoping to find someone who could help them understand what was happening in their home.

In June 1929, the Daily Mirror sent a reporter to Borley Rectory along with Harry Price, a well-known paranormal investigator. Price's initial investigation yielded immediate results. He witnessed objects being thrown, heard mysterious sounds, and observed a variety of other inexplicable occurrences. His reports and the newspaper articles brought Borley Rectory into the national spotlight, cementing its reputation as a haunted house.

After the Smiths left Borley Rectory, the house stood vacant for a short period before Reverend Lionel Foyster, a cousin of the Bulls, moved in with his wife, Marianne, and their adopted daughter in 1930. The Foyster family's experiences at Borley were even more intense and alarming. The hauntings escalated to include violent poltergeist activity, such as bottles being thrown, windows shattering, and mysterious fires breaking out. Reverend Foyster himself recorded a detailed account of the phenomena, which included Marian being slapped by unseen hands, objects disappearing and reappearing, and stones being thrown. One of the most disturbing aspects of the haunting involved Marianne being thrown from her bed and mysterious messages directed to her appearing on the walls.

The Foysters' tenure at Borley Rectory was marked by numerous attempts to exorcise the spirits, all of which proved unsuccessful. Eventually, due to the increasing intensity of the phenomena and Marianne's deteriorating health, the Foysters left the rectory in 1935. The house remained empty for several years, during which it fell into disrepair.

Harry Price returned to Borley Rectory in 1937, this time leasing the property for a full year to conduct an extensive investigation. He assembled a team of 48 researchers, including students and colleagues, to monitor the house for any signs of paranormal activity. Price's investigation was meticulously documented, and he published his findings in the book "The Most Haunted House in England." His team recorded numerous instances of unexplained phenomena, such as ghostly apparitions, mysterious lights, and objects moving without explanation. One of the most famous incidents involved the sighting of a ghostly nun seen through the rectory windows.

Despite Price's efforts, his investigations at Borley Rectory were met with skepticism. Critics accused him of fabricating evidence and manipulating the events to fit his narrative. Some claimed that the phenomena were the result of natural causes or even pranks by the residents themselves. Nevertheless, Price's work at Borley Rectory left a lasting legacy in the field of paranormal research and contributed to the house's enduring reputation as a haunted location.

In 1939, Borley Rectory was severely damaged by a fire. The fire was believed to have been caused by an oil lamp accident, although some speculated that it was the result of paranormal activity. The building was subsequently demolished in 1944, but the legend of Borley Rectory lived on. Even after its destruction, the site continued to attract paranormal investigators and enthusiasts, drawn by the tales of ghostly apparitions and unexplained phenomena.

In the years following the rectory's demolition, further investigations were conducted at the site and in the surrounding area. Many reported experiencing strange occurrences, including unexplained cold spots, disembodied voices, and sightings of ghostly figures. Despite the lack of a physical structure, the haunting seemed to persist, adding to the mystique of Borley Rectory.

Critics of the Borley Rectory hauntings have suggested various explanations for the phenomena. Some believe that the reports were exaggerated or fabricated by the residents, particularly Harry Price, to gain fame and notoriety. Others argue that the supernatural events were the result of natural causes, such as drafts, settling foundations, or the power of suggestion. The psychological state of the residents, particularly Marianne Foyster, has also been scrutinized, with some suggesting that the stress and isolation of living in a remote, reputedly haunted house may have contributed to the experiences.

Despite the skepticism, the Borley Rectory hauntings remain one of the most famous and debated cases in the history of paranormal investigation. The story has been the subject of numerous books, documentaries, and films, and continues to captivate those interested in the supernatural. The combination of historical intrigue, personal tragedy, and intense paranormal activity makes the Borley Rectory hauntings a compelling and enduring mystery.

In exploring the legacy of Borley Rectory, it is important to consider the broader cultural and historical context of the time. The early 20th century was a period of heightened interest in spiritualism and the supernatural, with many people seeking answers to life's mysteries through séances, mediums, and ghost hunting. The popularity of spiritualism provided a fertile ground for stories of haunted houses and ghostly apparitions, and Borley Rectory fit neatly into this cultural milieu.

The Borley Rectory hauntings also highlight the complexities of investigating paranormal phenomena. The subjective nature of many of the experiences, coupled with the lack of concrete evidence, makes it difficult to draw definitive conclusions. The case serves as a reminder of the challenges faced by paranormal investigators and the importance of maintaining a critical and open-minded approach to the study of the supernatural.

Chapter 16: The Mothman of Point Pleasant

The Mothman of Point Pleasant is a legend that has intrigued and mystified people since the 1960s. This enigmatic creature, described as a man-like figure with large, glowing red eyes and wings like a giant moth, first appeared in the small town of Point Pleasant, West Virginia. The Mothman sightings are deeply intertwined with local folklore, tragic events, and a legacy of fear and fascination that endures to this day.

The first recorded sighting of the Mothman occurred on November 12, 1966, when five men were digging a grave in a cemetery near Clendenin, West Virginia. They reported seeing a man-like figure with wings flying low over their heads. Just three days later, on November 15, 1966, two young couples—Roger and Linda Scarberry, and Steve and Mary Mallette—were driving near an abandoned TNT plant north of Point Pleasant. They claimed to have seen a large, gray creature with glowing red eyes standing in the middle of the road. According to their accounts, the creature spread its wings and took off, flying alongside their car at speeds of up to 100 miles per hour. Terrified, they drove to the local police station to report what they had seen.

These initial sightings sparked a wave of reports from other residents who claimed to have seen the Mothman. Over the next year, there were over 100 reported sightings, often describing the creature as standing between six and seven feet tall with a wingspan of ten feet. Witnesses consistently noted its hypnotic red eyes, which seemed to instill an overwhelming sense of fear and dread. These encounters typically took place around the TNT plant, a World War II-era munitions manufacturing and storage site, now abandoned and overgrown.

The Mothman sightings were accompanied by other strange phenomena. Witnesses reported seeing mysterious lights in the sky, hearing disembodied voices, and experiencing electrical disturbances. Many believed that the Mothman was a harbinger of doom, a supernatural being sent to warn of impending disaster. This belief seemed to be validated on December 15, 1967, when the Silver Bridge, which connected Point Pleasant to Gallipolis, Ohio, suddenly collapsed during rush hour traffic. The disaster resulted in the deaths of 46 people and was later attributed to the failure of a single eyebar in a suspension chain. However, many locals saw the bridge collapse as a direct correlation to the Mothman sightings, interpreting it as the catastrophe the creature had been forewarning.

The collapse of the Silver Bridge marked the end of the most intense period of Mothman sightings. In the aftermath, the story of the Mothman began to fade, but it was far from forgotten. In 1975, journalist and author John Keel published "The Mothman Prophecies," a book that linked the Mothman sightings to other unexplained phenomena in the area, including UFO sightings and encounters with Men in Black. Keel's work helped to cement the Mothman legend in popular culture, suggesting that the creature was part of a broader pattern of supernatural and extraterrestrial activity.

Keel's book also introduced the idea that the Mothman was not merely a cryptid, but perhaps an interdimensional being or a manifestation of some larger, more complex phenomenon. He proposed that the creature's appearance was connected to a series of bizarre and unsettling events in Point Pleasant, including phone calls with strange beeps and electronic disturbances, which he experienced firsthand. Keel's theories and the mysterious nature of the sightings added layers of intrigue and complexity to the Mothman legend.

In the decades since the Silver Bridge collapse, the Mothman has become a cultural icon. Point Pleasant has embraced its eerie legacy, hosting an annual Mothman Festival that attracts thousands of visitors from around the world. The festival features guest speakers, exhibits, vendors, and a guided bus tour of notable Mothman sighting locations. The Mothman Museum, located in downtown Point Pleasant, showcases memorabilia, eyewitness accounts, and historical artifacts related to the legend. The town also erected a twelve-foot-tall stainless-steel statue of the Mothman, created by artist Bob Roach, which stands as a testament to the creature's enduring presence in the community's collective memory.

Several theories have been proposed to explain the Mothman sightings. Skeptics often suggest that the creature could have been a large bird, such as a sandhill crane or an owl, whose unusual appearance and behavior were misinterpreted by frightened witnesses. The TNT plant area, with its labyrinth of tunnels and abandoned structures, could have provided a suitable habitat for such birds. The glowing red eyes described by witnesses might have been the result of eyeshine, a phenomenon common in many animals, where light is reflected from the retina.

Another theory posits that the Mothman was a product of mass hysteria, fueled by the tense atmosphere of the Cold War era and the proximity of the TNT plant, which may have heightened local fears of contamination or other dangers. Psychological factors, such as suggestion and expectation, could have played a significant role in shaping the witnesses' perceptions and accounts. The presence of John Keel and other investigators, along with the extensive media coverage, may have amplified these effects, creating a feedback loop that reinforced the belief in the Mothman.

Some researchers have explored the possibility that the Mothman sightings were part of a larger pattern of high strangeness, involving UFOs, poltergeist activity, and other anomalous phenomena. This theory suggests that Point Pleasant was a hotspot for unexplained occurrences, and that the Mothman was one manifestation of a broader, interconnected web of mysteries. This perspective draws on the work of researchers like Keel, who documented similar clusters of phenomena in other parts of the world, suggesting that these events might be linked by unknown forces or entities.

Despite the numerous theories and investigations, the true nature of the Mothman remains elusive. No definitive evidence has been found to explain the sightings conclusively, and the creature's origin and purpose continue to be subjects of speculation and debate. The Mothman legend endures not only because of the mystery and fear it evokes, but also because it taps into deeper themes of human experience—our fascination with the unknown, our need to find meaning in chaos, and our capacity for wonder and imagination.

In recent years, the Mothman has inspired a variety of media, including books, movies, and television shows. The 2002 film "The Mothman Prophecies," loosely based on John Keel's book, brought the story to a wider audience and introduced new generations to the legend. The film, starring Richard Gere and Laura Linney, dramatized the events in Point Pleasant and explored themes of fear, destiny, and the supernatural. It contributed to the Mothman's status as a pop culture icon and sparked renewed interest in the legend.

The Mothman's influence extends beyond Point Pleasant, as similar sightings have been reported in other parts of the world. For example, during the 2010s, there were several reports of a Mothman-like creature in Chicago, Illinois. Witnesses described seeing a large, winged humanoid with glowing red eyes, reminiscent of the original Mothman sightings. These reports have sparked debates among cryptozoologists, paranormal investigators, and skeptics, who continue to search for explanations and connections to the Point Pleasant legend.

The Mothman of Point Pleasant is a multifaceted legend that captures the imagination and continues to provoke curiosity and debate. It is a story that weaves together elements of folklore, tragedy, and the supernatural, creating a rich tapestry of mystery and wonder. Whether viewed as a cryptid, an interdimensional being, or a psychological phenomenon, the Mothman remains a powerful symbol of the unknown and the enduring human quest to understand the mysteries that lie beyond the veil of our everyday reality.

Chapter 17: The Smurl Family Haunting

The Smurl Family Haunting is one of the most compelling and controversial cases of alleged paranormal activity in American history. The events that reportedly plagued the Smurl family in their modest home in West Pittston, Pennsylvania, during the 1970s and 1980s, have been the subject of intense scrutiny, debate, and media attention. The haunting involved a series of disturbing and inexplicable phenomena, including poltergeist activity, demonic apparitions, and physical attacks, which purportedly affected multiple members of the family. The Smurl haunting stands out not only because of the severity and duration of the reported incidents but also because of the involvement of famous demonologists Ed and Lorraine Warren, whose investigation brought the case to national prominence.

The Smurl family consisted of Jack and Janet Smurl, their four daughters, and Jack's parents, John and Mary Smurl. In 1973, the family moved into a duplex in West Pittston, hoping for a fresh start. The house, built in 1896, seemed ideal for their needs, providing enough space for both families to live comfortably. However, shortly after moving in, the Smurls began to experience a series of unusual and increasingly disturbing occurrences.

Initially, the phenomena were relatively benign. Objects would go missing and reappear in odd places, and there were unexplained noises such as footsteps, knocks, and whispers. These early incidents were unsettling but not necessarily frightening, and the Smurls attempted to rationalize them. However, as time went on, the activity escalated in both frequency and intensity, taking a severe toll on the family's physical and mental well-being.

One of the first major incidents occurred in 1974 when the Smurls' television set burst into flames without any apparent cause. Despite being relatively new, the television inexplicably malfunctioned, filling the house with smoke. This event was followed by a series of plumbing problems, foul odors, and the sound of pig-like grunts echoing through the house. Janet Smurl reported feeling an invisible force touch her, and there were instances where family members felt unseen hands caressing them.

As the months turned into years, the activity grew more malevolent. Dark, shadowy figures were seen moving through the house, and the Smurls' daughters claimed to have seen grotesque faces staring at them from the darkness. Physical assaults also began to occur, with Jack and Janet both experiencing violent attacks from unseen forces. Janet was thrown from her bed and down the stairs on multiple occasions, and Jack was reportedly sexually assaulted by a succubus, a demonic entity believed to seduce men.

The Smurls sought help from various sources, including their local Catholic church, which performed multiple blessings on the house. Unfortunately, these efforts seemed to have little effect, and the activity continued unabated. Desperate for a solution, the family reached out to Ed and Lorraine Warren in 1986. The Warrens were renowned paranormal investigators and self-proclaimed demonologists, known for their involvement in high-profile cases such as the Amityville Horror.

The Warrens conducted a thorough investigation of the Smurl house, documenting their findings and attempting to communicate with the entities responsible for the haunting. According to the Warrens, the house was infested with several spirits, including a powerful and malevolent demon. They claimed that the demon had latched onto the Smurl family and was feeding off their fear and suffering. The Warrens performed a series of exorcisms and blessings, but the demonic activity persisted.

One of the most terrifying incidents reported by the Warrens occurred when Lorraine Warren, a clairvoyant, claimed to have seen the demonic entity manifest in front of her. She described it as a dark, amorphous mass with a face that was "a mixture of human and animal features." Despite their best efforts, the Warrens were unable to permanently expel the demon from the Smurl house, leading them to conclude that the family needed a more powerful intervention.

The Smurls' plight attracted significant media attention, leading to numerous articles, television appearances, and even a book co-authored by Ed and Lorraine Warren titled "The Haunted." The book detailed the events that the Smurl family had endured and the Warrens' investigation. In 1991, the story was adapted into a television movie called "The Haunted," further cementing the case's place in popular culture.

However, the Smurl haunting was not without its skeptics. Critics argued that the family's claims were either exaggerated or fabricated, suggesting that the Warrens had a vested interest in promoting the story to enhance their reputation and financial gain. Some pointed to inconsistencies in the accounts provided by the Smurls and the lack of concrete evidence to support the more extraordinary claims. Others speculated that the reported phenomena could be explained by psychological factors, environmental issues, or even outright hoaxes.

In response to the skepticism, the Smurl family maintained that their experiences were genuine and that they had no reason to lie. They pointed to the toll that the haunting had taken on their lives, including the physical and emotional distress they had endured. Despite the controversies, the Smurls' story resonated with many people, particularly those who had experienced similar unexplained phenomena.

The Smurl family eventually moved out of the duplex in 1987, hoping to leave the haunting behind. However, they claimed that the demonic presence followed them to their new home, although the activity was reportedly less intense. Over time, the media attention faded, and the Smurl haunting became another chapter in the annals of paranormal lore.

The legacy of the Smurl family haunting raises important questions about the nature of paranormal phenomena and the human capacity for belief and skepticism. For some, the Smurl case is a compelling example of the existence of supernatural forces and the power of faith and resilience in the face of darkness. For others, it is a cautionary tale about the dangers of credulity and the influence of sensationalism in shaping public perception.

The Smurl family haunting also highlights the challenges faced by paranormal investigators in proving the existence of supernatural entities. The subjective nature of many reported experiences, combined with the lack of definitive scientific evidence, makes it difficult to draw firm conclusions about cases like the Smurl haunting. This ambiguity is both a source of fascination and frustration for those who seek to understand the mysteries of the paranormal.

In the years since the Smurl haunting, the field of paranormal investigation has continued to evolve, incorporating new technologies and methodologies in an effort to capture and analyze evidence of unexplained phenomena. However, the fundamental questions raised by the Smurl case—about the nature of belief, the reliability of eyewitness testimony, and the limits of human understanding—remain as relevant as ever.

Ultimately, the story of the Smurl family haunting is a powerful reminder of the enduring allure of the unknown and the complex interplay between fear, faith, and the search for truth. Whether one views the Smurl haunting as a genuine encounter with the supernatural or as a product of psychological and social factors, it remains a compelling and thought-provoking case that continues to captivate and challenge our perceptions of reality.

Chapter 18: The Ghosts of the RMS Queen Mary

The RMS Queen Mary is an iconic ocean liner that sailed the North Atlantic Ocean from 1936 to 1967 for the Cunard-White Star Line. Known for its elegant Art Deco design and luxurious accommodations, the Queen Mary was a marvel of maritime engineering and a symbol of British pride. However, it is not just its storied past as a transatlantic passenger ship and wartime troop transport that has cemented its place in history. Since being permanently moored in Long Beach, California, the Queen Mary has become famous for an entirely different reason: its reputation as one of the most haunted places in the world. The ship is said to be home to a host of spectral inhabitants, with numerous reports of ghostly encounters, mysterious sounds, and unexplained phenomena that have captivated paranormal enthusiasts and researchers for decades.

The Queen Mary's haunted history begins with its construction and early years of service. Built by John Brown & Company in Clydebank, Scotland, the ship was launched on September 26, 1934, and made its maiden voyage on May 27, 1936. During its service, the Queen Mary hosted some of the world's most famous and affluent passengers, including royalty, Hollywood celebrities, and political figures. However, its career was not without tragedy. During World War II, the Queen Mary was converted into a troopship, dubbed the "Grey Ghost" due to its camouflaged paint. It played a crucial role in transporting soldiers, and its capacity to carry up to 16,000 troops at a time made it a vital asset. The ship's wartime service saw several deaths, including an accident in 1942 when it collided with the HMS Curacoa, resulting in the loss of over 300 lives.

One of the most infamous areas of the Queen Mary is the engine room, located 50 feet below water level, which is often described as the heart of the ship. This area has been the site of numerous reports of paranormal activity. One of the most frequently reported apparitions is that of a young engineer named John Pedder, who tragically died in 1966 after being crushed by a watertight door during a routine drill. Visitors have reported seeing a figure in blue overalls lurking near the door where Pedder was killed, and many have heard inexplicable banging noises and disembodied voices.

The ship's first-class swimming pool is another hotspot for ghostly encounters. Though it has been closed for decades, this pool area is said to be haunted by the spirits of women in 1930s-style bathing suits and little girls with their mothers. One of the most well-known apparitions is that of a young girl named Jackie, who is believed to have drowned in the second-class pool during the ship's service years. Witnesses have reported hearing the sound of a child giggling, splashing in the water, and calling for her mother. Jackie's ghost is often described as playful and mischievous, and she has been known to interact with visitors, sometimes even responding to questions.

The Queen Mary's elegant first-class staterooms and suites also have their share of ghostly guests. Stateroom B340, in particular, has garnered a reputation as one of the most haunted places on the ship. Guests who have stayed in this room have reported a wide range of strange occurrences, including faucets turning on and off by themselves, sheets being pulled off the bed, and the feeling of being watched. Some have even claimed to have seen a dark figure standing at the foot of the bed. The room was eventually closed to the public for many years due to the number of complaints and the intensity of the reported activity, but it has since been reopened for those brave enough to spend the night.

The ship's main deck is another area where paranormal activity has been frequently reported. The sounds of ghostly footsteps, distant voices, and the eerie feeling of being followed are common experiences for visitors walking along the deck. Some have even claimed to see apparitions of crew members dressed in old-fashioned uniforms, going about their duties as if they were still on a transatlantic voyage.

The ship's bow, where the Queen Mary collided with the HMS Curacoa, is said to be haunted by the spirits of those who perished in the accident. Visitors have reported hearing the sounds of metal scraping against metal, cries for help, and the feeling of intense sadness and despair. The lingering presence of those lost souls is believed to be a residual haunting, a kind of psychic imprint left by the traumatic event.

In addition to these specific locations, there are countless other reports of paranormal activity throughout the ship. Shadowy figures, unexplained cold spots, and the feeling of being touched by unseen hands are just some of the phenomena experienced by those who have visited the Queen Mary. The ship has been investigated by numerous paranormal researchers and featured on television shows such as "Ghost Hunters" and "Most Haunted," all of which have documented a variety of strange occurrences.

One of the most comprehensive investigations of the Queen Mary's paranormal activity was conducted by Peter James, a renowned psychic and paranormal investigator. James spent many years exploring the ship and communicating with its ghostly residents. He famously made contact with the spirit of the little girl Jackie, and his recordings of their interactions have become some of the most compelling pieces of evidence of the ship's hauntings. James also reported encountering other spirits, including that of John Pedder and various unnamed entities.

The Queen Mary's ghostly reputation has made it a popular destination for tourists and paranormal enthusiasts. The ship offers a variety of ghost tours and paranormal investigation experiences, allowing visitors to explore its haunted history firsthand. These tours often include visits to the most active areas of the ship, and many participants have reported their own ghostly encounters during these excursions.

The Queen Mary's hauntings are a fascinating blend of history, tragedy, and the supernatural. The ship's long and storied past, combined with the numerous reports of paranormal activity, has created an enduring legend that continues to captivate and intrigue. Whether one is a believer in the supernatural or a skeptic, the tales of ghostly apparitions, mysterious sounds, and unexplained phenomena aboard the Queen Mary offer a glimpse into the unknown and the enduring mystery of what lies beyond.

The allure of the Queen Mary's ghost stories is not just about the fear of the unknown but also about the connection to the past. The spirits that are said to haunt the ship are a reminder of the countless lives that were touched by the Queen Mary, from the glamorous passengers of its golden years to the brave soldiers of World War II. Each reported sighting and unexplained phenomenon add another layer to the ship's rich tapestry of history and mystery.

As the Queen Mary continues to serve as a hotel and tourist attraction, the stories of its ghostly inhabitants live on. The ship's unique blend of luxury, history, and the paranormal ensures that it remains a compelling destination for those seeking to experience a piece of the past—and perhaps catch a glimpse of the otherworldly. The RMS Queen Mary stands as a testament to the enduring power of ghost stories and the human fascination with the mysteries that lie beyond our understanding. Whether one believes in ghosts or not, the legends of the Queen Mary offer a captivating journey into the unknown, where history and the supernatural intertwine in a hauntingly beautiful way.

Chapter 19: The Sallie House

The Sallie House is one of the most infamous haunted locations in the United States, attracting paranormal investigators, thrill-seekers, and curious visitors from around the world. Located in Atchison, Kansas, the house has a history that dates back to the early 20th century, and its dark and eerie past has given rise to numerous chilling stories and accounts of paranormal activity.

The legend of the Sallie House began in the early 1900s when a young girl named Sallie was allegedly brought to the house, which then served as the residence and practice of a local physician, Dr. Charles Finney. According to the story, Sallie was suffering from severe abdominal pain, which was later diagnosed as appendicitis. Dr. Finney decided that immediate surgery was necessary to save the girl's life. However, due to the urgency of the situation, the doctor began the operation before the anesthesia had fully taken effect, causing Sallie to experience excruciating pain. Tragically, Sallie died on the operating table, and it is believed that her spirit remained in the house, seeking justice for the pain and suffering she endured.

The house remained relatively quiet until the early 1990s when Tony and Debra Pickman moved in. The couple was initially unaware of the house's haunted reputation but soon began to experience strange and unexplainable occurrences. Debra, who was pregnant at the time, reported feeling an overwhelming sense of unease, and the couple's dog would bark incessantly at seemingly empty spaces. Over time, the activity escalated. They witnessed objects moving on their own, unexplained cold spots, and even apparitions. One of the most disturbing events involved their infant son, Taylor. The Pickmans found strange scratches and burns on the baby's body, which they could not explain. Tony also experienced physical attacks, including scratches, bites, and burns that appeared spontaneously.

As the paranormal activity continued, the Pickmans sought help from various paranormal investigators and psychics. One psychic medium identified the presence of a young girl named Sallie and suggested that she was responsible for the disturbances. However, the medium also sensed a darker, more malevolent presence in the house, which she believed was manipulating Sallie's spirit. This duality of presences added another layer of complexity to the hauntings and deepened the mystery surrounding the Sallie House.

The house gained national attention after being featured on several television shows, including "Sightings," "Unsolved Mysteries," and "Ghost Adventures." Paranormal investigators who visited the house reported experiencing a wide range of phenomena, from unexplained noises and voices to physical attacks and the sensation of being watched. Equipment failures and drained batteries were also common, adding to the house's reputation as a hotspot for paranormal activity. During investigations, many reported capturing EVPs (Electronic Voice Phenomena), mysterious orbs, and shadowy figures on camera. Some investigators even claimed to have communicated with Sallie and other spirits through spirit boxes and other devices.

The Sallie House's notoriety continued to grow, attracting more visitors and investigators. Some have speculated that the house's history is much darker than originally believed, with theories suggesting that it may have been the site of occult practices or other sinister activities. Despite extensive investigations and numerous documented experiences, the true nature of the hauntings remains a subject of debate and speculation. Some skeptics argue that the experiences can be attributed to psychological factors, environmental conditions, or outright fabrication. However, the sheer volume of consistent reports from various sources over the years lends a degree of credibility to the claims of paranormal activity.

Today, the Sallie House stands as a chilling reminder of the unknown and the unexplained. It remains a popular destination for paranormal enthusiasts and a subject of fascination for those interested in the supernatural. The house is often rented out for overnight investigations, allowing people to experience its eerie atmosphere firsthand. Visitors often leave with their own stories of strange occurrences, further fueling the legend of the Sallie House. Despite the passage of time and countless investigations, the mystery of the Sallie House endures, continuing to captivate and terrify those who dare to explore its haunted halls.

The Sallie House's story is a compelling blend of historical tragedy, personal horror, and paranormal mystery. It serves as a potent reminder of the thin veil that separates the world of the living from the realm of the unknown. Whether one believes in the supernatural or not, the tales from the Sallie House provoke a sense of curiosity and unease, challenging our understanding of reality and the afterlife. The house remains an enigmatic presence in the paranormal community, its walls echoing with the whispers of the past and the unanswered questions that linger in its haunted rooms.

Chapter 20: The Ghost of Resurrection Mary

The legend of Resurrection Mary is one of Chicago's most famous and enduring ghost stories, captivating the imaginations of locals and visitors alike for decades. This spectral tale centers around a young woman named Mary, whose restless spirit is said to haunt the area near Resurrection Cemetery in Justice, Illinois, a southwestern suburb of Chicago. The story of Resurrection Mary is a blend of urban legend, personal accounts, and historical speculation, weaving together a narrative that continues to intrigue and mystify those who hear it.

The origins of the Resurrection Mary legend date back to the 1930s. According to the most popular version of the story, Mary was a beautiful young woman who spent an evening dancing with her boyfriend at the O. Henry Ballroom, a popular dance hall on Archer Avenue. After an argument with her boyfriend, Mary stormed out of the ballroom and decided to walk home along Archer Avenue. Tragically, she was struck by a car and killed instantly. Her grieving parents buried her in Resurrection Cemetery, clad in the white dress she had worn that fateful night. It is said that since her untimely death, her spirit has been seen wandering Archer Avenue, attempting to make her way back home or to the dance hall where she spent her last evening.

The first reported sightings of Resurrection Mary began in the late 1930s and have continued sporadically ever since. Witnesses describe seeing a young woman dressed in a white party dress, often with light blonde hair and blue eyes. She is usually seen hitchhiking along Archer Avenue, sometimes near the O. Henry Ballroom, now known as the Willowbrook Ballroom, and other times near Resurrection Cemetery. Drivers who pick her up report that she is usually quiet and reserved, providing minimal details about herself. In some accounts, she gives an address on the North Side of Chicago. However, when the driver reaches the cemetery gates, Mary vanishes without a trace, leaving the driver bewildered and often frightened.

One of the most famous encounters with Resurrection Mary occurred in the early 1970s when a cab driver named Ralph picked up a young woman near the old O. Henry Ballroom. According to Ralph's account, the woman was wearing a white dress and seemed distressed. She asked to be taken to a house in the nearby Bridgeport neighborhood. When Ralph arrived at the address, the woman had vanished from his cab. Puzzled, Ralph knocked on the door of the house and was informed by the elderly woman who answered that there was no young woman living there, and she had no idea who he was talking about. This incident, along with many similar stories, has contributed to the enduring legend of Resurrection Mary.

Another notable account involves Jerry Palus, who claimed to have danced with a girl named Mary at the Liberty Grove and Hall, a dance hall located on Chicago's south side, in 1939. According to Palus, they spent the evening dancing and having a good time. When he offered to drive her home, she directed him to Archer Avenue and asked to be let out near Resurrection Cemetery. As she exited the car and began walking toward the cemetery gates, she suddenly disappeared. Palus was so disturbed by the experience that he later visited Resurrection Cemetery and found a gravestone bearing the name Mary with the same last name she had given him that night.

The story of Resurrection Mary is not just confined to the accounts of those who have picked her up. Many people claim to have seen her walking along Archer Avenue, often near the cemetery gates. In some cases, she is seen standing on the side of the road, appearing lifelike until she suddenly vanishes. There have also been reports of Mary appearing inside the cemetery itself, sometimes seen standing behind the gates or near specific graves. One of the most eerie aspects of these sightings is the consistency in the descriptions of her appearance and behavior, suggesting that those who have seen her are witnessing the same spectral figure.

Skeptics and historians have tried to uncover the true identity of Resurrection Mary, speculating that she may be the ghost of a real person buried in Resurrection Cemetery. Several candidates have been proposed, including a young woman named Mary Bregovy, who died in a car accident in 1934, and another young woman named Mary Miskowski, who was killed by a hit-and-run driver in 1930. However, none of these theories have been definitively proven, and the true identity of Resurrection Mary remains a mystery.

Resurrection Cemetery itself adds to the eerie atmosphere surrounding the legend. Established in 1904, it is one of the largest cemeteries in the Chicago area, with over 150,000 graves. The cemetery's vast expanse of tombstones, mausoleums, and crypts provides a fitting backdrop for ghostly tales. Over the years, the cemetery has been the site of numerous reported paranormal activities, including unexplained lights, strange noises, and ghostly apparitions. Visitors to the cemetery often describe a feeling of unease and the sensation of being watched.

The legend of Resurrection Mary has permeated popular culture, inspiring books, songs, and even films. The story is frequently included in collections of ghost stories and urban legends, and it remains a popular topic for paranormal investigators and enthusiasts. Local tours often include stops at the sites associated with Mary, and her story is a staple of Halloween folklore in the Chicago area. Despite the passage of time, new sightings and encounters continue to be reported, keeping the legend alive and adding new layers to the mystery.

Whether one believes in the supernatural or not, the story of Resurrection Mary is a fascinating part of Chicago's cultural heritage. It serves as a reminder of the power of folklore and the enduring nature of ghost stories. The tale of a young woman who died tragically and continues to seek a ride home resonates with the universal themes of loss, longing, and the unknown. Resurrection Mary's story is a blend of tragedy, mystery, and the inexplicable, captivating the imagination and challenging our understanding of life and death.

The legend of Resurrection Mary endures as a testament to the human fascination with the unknown and the supernatural. Her ghostly presence on Archer Avenue and near Resurrection Cemetery continues to spark curiosity and fear, drawing people into the world of the unexplained. As new generations hear the tale and perhaps encounter Mary themselves, the story grows, cementing her place in the annals of paranormal lore. The ghost of Resurrection Mary remains a haunting and enigmatic figure, a spectral reminder of the mysteries that lie just beyond the veil of our understanding.

Chapter 21: The Haunted Island of Poveglia

Poveglia Island, located in the Venetian Lagoon between Venice and Lido in northern Italy, is often referred to as one of the most haunted places on Earth. The island's history is steeped in tragedy, death, and dark tales, making it a focal point for paranormal enthusiasts and ghost hunters from around the world. Its chilling past and the eerie remains left behind contribute to its reputation as a place of great supernatural significance.

The history of Poveglia Island dates back to Roman times, but it gained its sinister reputation much later. During the Roman Empire, the island was used as a place of exile for those suffering from the plague. This practice continued into the Middle Ages when the Black Death ravaged Europe. As one of the deadliest pandemics in human history, the Black Death killed an estimated 75-200 million people. Poveglia became a quarantine station where ships suspected of carrying the plague were docked, and the infected were brought to the island to live out their final days in isolation. The bodies of the deceased were often burned in large pits, and it is believed that the ashes of the dead make up a significant portion of the island's soil.

In the 18th century, during another outbreak of the plague, Poveglia's role as a quarantine island was reinforced. Thousands of people were sent there to die, and the island's macabre function as a dumping ground for the diseased and dying intensified. The remains of those who perished were buried in mass graves, and it is said that over 160,000 bodies ended up on the island. The air of death and despair that surrounded Poveglia during these times is a key element of its haunted reputation.

In 1922, Poveglia's dark history took another turn when the island became the site of a mental hospital. The asylum quickly gained a reputation for its inhumane treatment of patients. According to local legend, a particularly sadistic doctor performed crude lobotomies and other experimental treatments on the patients. He is said to have tortured and abused many of them, causing great suffering and leading to numerous deaths. The doctor himself supposedly met a grim fate when he fell—or was pushed— from the hospital's bell tower, driven mad by the spirits of his victims. His death did nothing to quell the tales of ghosts and restless spirits said to roam the island.

The asylum was closed in 1968, and the island was abandoned. Over the years, the decaying buildings and the pervasive sense of sorrow have added to the island's eerie atmosphere. Today, the remnants of the hospital, the plague pits, and other structures stand in ruins, overgrown by vegetation and shrouded in mystery. Poveglia is off-limits to casual visitors, but those who have ventured there report a range of paranormal phenomena, from ghostly apparitions to disembodied voices and inexplicable sounds.

Numerous paranormal investigators and ghost hunters have explored Poveglia, often documenting their experiences. Many report feeling an overwhelming sense of dread and sadness upon setting foot on the island. Some claim to have seen shadowy figures, heard screams, and felt unseen hands touching them. Electronic equipment often malfunctions, and strange, unexplainable noises are frequently recorded. These accounts reinforce the island's reputation as a place where the veil between the living and the dead is exceptionally thin.

One of the most compelling aspects of Poveglia's haunted reputation is the consistency of the reports. Visitors from different backgrounds and with varying levels of belief in the paranormal often describe similar experiences. This has led many to believe that the island's dark history has indeed left a lasting imprint, creating a hotspot for supernatural activity. The stories and legends surrounding Poveglia have been passed down through generations, further entrenching the island's status as a place of horror and intrigue.

The local Venetians have a strong aversion to Poveglia, often referring to it as "the island of ghosts." Fishermen avoid the waters around it, fearing bad luck or worse. The reluctance of locals to go near the island speaks volumes about its fearsome reputation. Even in a region rich with history and legend, Poveglia stands out as a place to be avoided.

Adding to the island's mystique are the many failed attempts to repurpose it. Over the years, various plans to develop the island into a resort or luxury property have been proposed and subsequently abandoned. Investors and developers often cite the island's haunted reputation as a deterrent, believing that its dark past would overshadow any new ventures. The abandoned nature of these projects contributes to the sense that Poveglia is cursed or beyond redemption.

Poveglia has also captured the attention of popular culture, featuring in various television shows, documentaries, and books. Its haunted history makes it a compelling subject for those interested in the supernatural, and it frequently appears in lists of the world's most haunted locations. These portrayals often emphasize the island's eerie atmosphere and tragic past, further solidifying its place in the public imagination as a haunted and forbidden place.

Despite the fascination with Poveglia, the Italian government remains protective of the island, limiting access to ensure the safety of potential visitors and to preserve the island's historical integrity. This restricted access only heightens the island's allure, making it a tantalizing but elusive destination for those drawn to the macabre.

The haunted island of Poveglia is a testament to the enduring power of history and legend. Its legacy as a place of suffering, death, and paranormal activity continues to captivate and terrify. Whether one believes in ghosts or not, the island's tragic past and the eerie experiences reported by those who have dared to visit create a compelling narrative that blurs the line between history and myth. Poveglia remains a potent symbol of the darker aspects of human experience, its haunted reputation serving as a stark reminder of the pain and suffering that once took place on its shores.

Chapter 22: The Chupacabra Sightings

The Chupacabra, a cryptid rooted in the folklore of Latin America, particularly Puerto Rico, Mexico, and the southwestern United States, has captivated the imagination and stirred fear since its first reported sightings in the 1990s. The creature's name, derived from the Spanish words "chupar," meaning "to suck," and "cabra," meaning "goat," reflects its infamous reputation for attacking livestock, particularly goats, and draining their blood. The legend of the Chupacabra has evolved over the years, blending elements of mystery, cultural folklore, and alleged eyewitness accounts to create a phenomenon that continues to intrigue and perplex both believers and skeptics alike.

The first reported sighting of the Chupacabra occurred in March 1995 in Puerto Rico. A farmer named Madelyne Tolentino claimed to have seen a strange creature near the town of Canóvanas. According to her description, the creature was unlike anything she had ever seen before. It was about three to four feet tall, with large, glowing red eyes, a row of spines running down its back, and long, clawed fingers. It stood on two legs and had a distinctly reptilian appearance. Shortly after her sighting, several reports emerged of livestock found dead and drained of blood, with puncture wounds on their necks. These incidents sparked widespread panic and speculation about the existence of a blood-sucking predator.

As news of the Chupacabra spread, more sightings and reports of livestock mutilations were documented across Puerto Rico. The creature became a subject of intense media coverage, with sensational stories and images circulating in newspapers and on television. People began to speculate about the origins of the Chupacabra, with theories ranging from a mutated animal to an extraterrestrial being. Some even suggested that the creature was the result of secret government experiments. The lack of concrete evidence and the mysterious nature of the attacks fueled the legend, making the Chupacabra a fixture in contemporary folklore.

The phenomenon soon spread beyond Puerto Rico. In the late 1990s and early 2000s, reports of Chupacabra sightings and livestock attacks began to emerge from other parts of Latin America, including Mexico, Chile, Brazil, and even the southern United States. Each new sighting added to the growing mythology of the Chupacabra, with variations in descriptions of the creature. In some accounts, it was described as having wings and the ability to fly, while others depicted it as a more canine or panther-like creature. Despite these variations, the core elements of the legend—blood-sucking attacks on livestock and a mysterious, elusive predator—remained consistent.

One of the most significant waves of Chupacabra sightings occurred in the early 2000s in Texas. Ranchers and farmers reported finding their livestock dead, with the same telltale puncture wounds and blood loss that characterized earlier attacks. The descriptions of the creature varied, but many witnesses described it as a hairless, dog-like animal with sharp teeth and claws. In some cases, carcasses of alleged Chupacabras were found, but upon examination, these often turned out to be coyotes or dogs suffering from severe mange, a skin disease that causes hair loss and a mangy appearance. Despite these findings, the legend persisted, and the Chupacabra continued to capture the public's imagination.

The Chupacabra phenomenon has also been linked to broader cultural and social contexts. In many ways, the legend of the Chupacabra reflects deep-seated fears and anxieties about the unknown and the uncontrollable. The attacks on livestock, a crucial resource for rural communities, symbolize a threat to economic stability and security. The creature's elusive nature and the inability to definitively identify or capture it mirror the uncertainties and challenges faced by these communities. Additionally, the spread of the Chupacabra legend through media and popular culture highlights the role of storytelling and myth-making in shaping perceptions and beliefs.

The Chupacabra has become a popular subject in various forms of media and entertainment. It has been featured in numerous books, movies, television shows, and even video games. These portrayals often emphasize the creature's terrifying and mysterious aspects, further embedding it in popular culture. Shows like "The X-Files" and "Destination Truth" have dedicated episodes to investigating the Chupacabra, blending fiction and alleged reality to create compelling narratives. These portrayals have helped to keep the legend alive and relevant, ensuring that the Chupacabra remains a topic of fascination for new generations.

Despite the widespread belief in the Chupacabra, scientific investigations have largely debunked the existence of such a creature. Biologists and wildlife experts argue that many of the sightings and attacks attributed to the Chupacabra can be explained by known animals and natural phenomena. The carcasses found are often identified as dogs, coyotes, or raccoons suffering from severe mange, which gives them a grotesque and unusual appearance. Additionally, the puncture wounds and blood loss in livestock can be caused by various predators, including dogs, coyotes, and even birds. The phenomenon of "chupacabras" can be seen as a modern myth, fueled by misidentifications, sensationalism, and the human propensity for storytelling.

One of the most comprehensive investigations into the Chupacabra legend was conducted by Benjamin Radford, a paranormal investigator and author. In his book "Tracking the Chupacabra," Radford examines the origins and evolution of the legend, as well as the various sightings and evidence associated with it. He concludes that the Chupacabra is a product of contemporary folklore, shaped by cultural influences, media sensationalism, and misidentifications. Radford's work provides a skeptical perspective on the phenomenon, highlighting the importance of critical thinking and scientific inquiry in understanding such legends.

Despite the lack of scientific evidence, the Chupacabra continues to be a powerful symbol in popular culture and folklore. It embodies the mystery and fear of the unknown, as well as the enduring human fascination with monsters and the supernatural. The legend of the Chupacabra serves as a reminder of the ways in which folklore can evolve and adapt, reflecting the changing fears and anxieties of society. Whether one believes in the existence of the Chupacabra or views it as a modern myth, its impact on contemporary culture is undeniable.

Chapter 23: The Legend of La Llorona

The Legend of La Llorona is one of the most enduring and haunting pieces of folklore in Latin American culture, with roots that stretch across Mexico, Central America, and the American Southwest. The story of La Llorona, or "The Weeping Woman," is a tale of love, betrayal, and tragic loss that has been passed down through generations, permeating the cultural consciousness and serving as a cautionary tale for children and adults alike. The legend is deeply intertwined with historical, cultural, and social contexts, and it has evolved over time to remain relevant in contemporary society.

At its core, the legend of La Llorona tells the story of a beautiful woman named Maria who falls in love with a wealthy man. They marry and have two children, but their happiness is short-lived. Maria's husband becomes unfaithful and leaves her for another woman, shattering her heart. In a fit of grief and rage, Maria takes her children to a river and drowns them. Almost immediately, she is overcome with remorse and despair, and she drowns herself as well. However, her soul is condemned to wander the earth, forever searching for her lost children. Her anguished cries, "Ay, mis hijos!" ("Oh, my children!"), are said to be heard near bodies of water, and it is believed that she kidnaps children who wander too close, mistaking them for her own.

The variations of the La Llorona story are numerous, reflecting the diverse cultures and communities that have embraced the legend. In some versions, Maria is portrayed as a victim of her circumstances, driven to madness by her husband's betrayal and her own grief. In others, she is depicted as a vengeful spirit, punishing those who come too near her watery domain. The details of the story may change, but the central themes of love, loss, and eternal sorrow remain consistent.

The origins of the La Llorona legend are difficult to pinpoint, but they likely date back to the early colonial period in Latin America. Some scholars suggest that the story may have pre-Hispanic roots, possibly connected to Aztec mythology. The Aztecs had a goddess named Cihuacoatl, also known as the Snake Woman, who was associated with motherhood and childbirth. Cihuacoatl was said to appear as a weeping woman, mourning the loss of her children. This pre-Columbian myth may have blended with Spanish and indigenous folklore to create the story of La Llorona as we know it today.

The La Llorona legend has served various social and cultural functions over the centuries. In many communities, it is used as a cautionary tale to keep children from wandering too far from home, particularly near bodies of water. Parents warn their children that if they do not behave or stay close, La Llorona will come for them. The story also serves as a moral lesson about the consequences of infidelity, betrayal, and uncontrolled emotions. It reflects societal attitudes towards women, motherhood, and family, often highlighting the pressures and expectations placed on women in traditional roles.

In addition to its role as a cautionary tale, the legend of La Llorona has also been interpreted as a symbol of collective trauma and loss. The story resonates with the experiences of many Latin American communities, particularly those that have faced colonization, displacement, and violence. La Llorona's endless search for her children can be seen as a metaphor for the enduring grief and longing of those who have lost loved ones to war, migration, or other forms of suffering. The legend provides a way to process and express these deep-seated emotions, offering a form of catharsis and communal healing.

The enduring power of the La Llorona legend is evident in its continued presence in contemporary culture. The story has been adapted into numerous films, television shows, books, and even music. In the United States, the legend has become a part of the broader cultural tapestry, particularly in areas with large Hispanic populations. Movies like "The Curse of La Llorona" (2019) have brought the story to a global audience, blending horror with traditional folklore. These adaptations often emphasize the terrifying aspects of the legend, portraying La Llorona as a malevolent ghost who preys on the living.

Despite the sensationalized portrayals in popular media, the legend of La Llorona retains its cultural significance and resonance. It continues to be a source of inspiration for artists, writers, and performers, who explore its themes in various creative forms. The story's ability to evoke strong emotions and address universal human experiences ensures its lasting relevance. La Llorona remains a powerful symbol of grief, loss, and the complexities of human emotion, transcending cultural and temporal boundaries.

The legend of La Llorona also intersects with issues of gender and identity. The story often reflects the struggles and challenges faced by women, particularly in patriarchal societies. La Llorona's tragic fate can be seen as a commentary on the limited options available to women and the harsh consequences of societal expectations. Her transformation into a weeping ghost underscores the enduring impact of grief and loss, highlighting the ways in which women's voices and experiences are often marginalized or silenced.

In contemporary discussions of folklore and mythology, La Llorona is frequently analyzed through feminist and intersectional lenses. Scholars and activists explore how the legend both reinforces and challenges traditional gender roles, as well as how it intersects with issues of race, class, and cultural identity. La Llorona's story is reinterpreted and reimagined in ways that reflect the evolving concerns and perspectives of modern society. This ongoing reinterpretation ensures that the legend remains dynamic and relevant, adapting to the changing cultural landscape.

In addition to its cultural and social significance, the legend of La Llorona has also inspired various forms of artistic expression. Visual artists depict La Llorona in paintings, murals, and sculptures, often emphasizing her sorrowful and haunting presence. Writers and poets explore the emotional depth of her story, using it as a framework to address themes of love, loss, and redemption. Musicians create songs that capture the eerie and melancholic tone of the legend, blending traditional folk music with contemporary styles. These artistic interpretations contribute to the rich tapestry of La Llorona's legacy, ensuring that her story continues to resonate with audiences across different media.

La Llorona's influence extends beyond Latin American communities, becoming a part of the broader cultural imagination. The story is shared and retold in diverse contexts, reflecting its universal appeal and emotional impact. La Llorona's tale of love, betrayal, and eternal mourning speaks to fundamental human experiences, transcending cultural and geographical boundaries. Her legend serves as a reminder of the enduring power of folklore to shape our understanding of the world and to connect us to our shared humanity.

Chapter 24: The Jersey Devil Encounters

The legend of the Jersey Devil, a creature said to inhabit the Pine Barrens of southern New Jersey, is one of the most enduring and intriguing pieces of American folklore. Described as a winged beast with the head of a horse, the body of a kangaroo, horns, small arms with clawed hands, and a long, forked tail, the Jersey Devil has been the subject of countless sightings, tales, and investigations since the 18th century. The creature's origins, its various reported encounters, and the cultural impact it has had over the centuries contribute to a rich and compelling narrative that blends history, myth, and mystery.

The origins of the Jersey Devil legend date back to the early 1700s. According to the most popular version of the story, the creature was born to a woman named Deborah Leeds in 1735. Deborah, already a mother of twelve children, cursed the thirteenth child in frustration, declaring it would be the devil. When the child was born, it transformed into a monstrous creature with hooves, a goat's head, bat wings, and a forked tail. The beast let out a blood-curdling scream and flew up the chimney, disappearing into the Pine Barrens, where it has been said to roam ever since.

The Leeds family, prominent in southern New Jersey, is often linked to the origin of the Jersey Devil legend. Daniel Leeds, an early settler, was known for his involvement in political and religious controversies, which may have contributed to the creation of the legend. His almanac publications and disputes with the Quaker community of the time could have provided fertile ground for the myth's development, intertwining real historical figures with supernatural lore. The Leeds family's coat of arms, which included dragon-like creatures, further fueled the association between the family and the legend of the Jersey Devil.

Over the centuries, numerous sightings and encounters with the Jersey Devil have been reported, contributing to its notoriety. One of the earliest documented sightings occurred in 1820, when Commodore Stephen Decatur, a naval hero, reportedly saw a strange creature while testing cannonballs at the Hanover Mill Works. Decatur claimed to have fired a cannonball directly at the creature, but it had no effect. Another prominent account from the 19th century involved Joseph Bonaparte, the elder brother of Napoleon Bonaparte and former king of Spain, who allegedly encountered the Jersey Devil while hunting in the Pine Barrens in 1820.

The most intense period of reported sightings occurred in January 1909, when the Jersey Devil was allegedly seen by hundreds of people across New Jersey and southeastern Pennsylvania. This week-long event, known as the "Phenomenal Week," included sightings by police officers, firefighters, and residents who described a flying creature with glowing eyes. Newspapers of the time published sensational reports, and the sightings led to widespread panic. Schools closed, and factories shut down as fear of the Jersey Devil spread. Tracks attributed to the creature were found in the snow, adding to the hysteria.

Descriptions of the Jersey Devil during this period were remarkably consistent, typically involving a flying, winged beast with a distinctive scream. Reports included the creature attacking a trolley car in Haddon Heights and a social club in Camden, as well as police officers shooting at it without any effect. The flurry of sightings in 1909 remains one of the most significant episodes in the legend's history, cementing the Jersey Devil's status in American folklore.

In the decades that followed, sightings of the Jersey Devil continued, albeit less frequently. In 1927, a cab driver in Salem City claimed to have encountered the creature while changing a tire. In 1930, a group of people in Clayton reportedly saw the Jersey Devil while ice skating. Throughout the 1950s and 1960s, sightings were sporadic but persistent, often reported by hunters, farmers, and travelers in the Pine Barrens. These encounters typically involved fleeting glimpses of the creature or hearing its distinctive scream.

The Jersey Devil's legend has been bolstered by its impact on local culture and tourism. The Pine Barrens, a dense forested area with a reputation for being eerie and mysterious, provides a fitting backdrop for tales of the supernatural. The region's isolation and unique environment have contributed to its association with the paranormal. Over time, the Jersey Devil has become a symbol of the Pine Barrens, with local businesses, sports teams, and festivals adopting its name and imagery. The New Jersey Devils, a professional hockey team, are named in honor of the creature, further embedding the legend in the state's cultural identity.

In addition to its local significance, the Jersey Devil has captured the imagination of the broader public. The creature has been featured in various forms of media, including books, television shows, and films. In the realm of cryptozoology, the study of animals whose existence is not recognized by mainstream science, the Jersey Devil is a prominent figure. Enthusiasts and researchers continue to investigate sightings and gather evidence, although no definitive proof of the creature's existence has been found.

One of the more intriguing aspects of the Jersey Devil legend is its adaptability and persistence. Despite the lack of concrete evidence, the story has endured and evolved, reflecting changing cultural and social contexts. In modern times, the legend has been subject to skepticism and scientific scrutiny. Explanations for sightings often involve misidentifications of known animals, such as large birds or deer, or psychological factors, including the power of suggestion and mass hysteria. Nevertheless, the allure of the Jersey Devil endures, fueled by the mystery and fear that surround the unknown.

The Pine Barrens themselves have contributed to the mystique of the Jersey Devil. This vast, sparsely populated region, with its dense forests, swamps, and unique ecosystem, has long been associated with folklore and legends. The Pine Barrens have been the setting for various tales of ghosts, witches, and other supernatural phenomena, creating a rich tapestry of stories that intertwine with the legend of the Jersey Devil. The region's geography, with its labyrinthine paths and remote areas, provides an ideal setting for a creature to remain hidden from the prying eyes of civilization.

In recent years, the Jersey Devil has continued to capture the public's imagination, thanks in part to the rise of paranormal investigation shows and internet forums dedicated to cryptozoology and the supernatural. Shows like "MonsterQuest" and "The X-Files" have featured episodes exploring the legend, bringing it to a wider audience. The internet has provided a platform for enthusiasts to share stories, sightings, and theories, keeping the legend alive and vibrant. Social media, in particular, has allowed for the rapid dissemination of reports and speculation, ensuring that the Jersey Devil remains a topic of interest and debate.

The legend of the Jersey Devil also serves as a lens through which to explore broader themes in American folklore. It reflects a fascination with the unknown and the monstrous, a desire to explain and rationalize the unexplained, and a need to create and perpetuate stories that speak to our deepest fears and curiosities. The Jersey Devil, like other legendary creatures, represents the intersection of history, myth, and human imagination. It is a testament to the power of storytelling and the enduring appeal of the mysterious and the supernatural.

Chapter 25: The Haunted Myrtles Plantation

The Myrtles Plantation, located in St. Francisville, Louisiana, is widely regarded as one of the most haunted houses in America. Its history is steeped in tales of tragedy, murder, and the supernatural. Built in 1796 by General David Bradford, also known as "Whiskey Dave," the plantation has accumulated a reputation for being a hotbed of paranormal activity. The stories associated with the Myrtles Plantation are numerous, ranging from ghostly apparitions to unexplained phenomena, and they have made it a popular destination for ghost hunters and curious tourists alike.

The history of the Myrtles Plantation is as intriguing as it is tragic. General David Bradford, a successful lawyer and businessman, fled his home in Pennsylvania after his involvement in the Whiskey Rebellion, a protest against the federal excise tax on whiskey. Seeking refuge, Bradford purchased 600 acres of land in Louisiana and began constructing the plantation. Initially named "Laurel Grove," the estate changed hands several times, each new owner adding to its storied past.

One of the most enduring legends associated with the Myrtles Plantation is the story of Chloe, a slave who worked in the household of Clark Woodruff, one of the plantation's early owners. According to legend, Chloe was caught eavesdropping on Woodruff's conversations and, as punishment, had one of her ears cut off. To hide her mutilation, she wore a green turban. Seeking revenge, Chloe allegedly poisoned a birthday cake intended for Woodruff's daughters, killing two of his children and his wife, Sara. In retaliation, Chloe was hanged by her fellow slaves and thrown into the Mississippi River. The ghost of Chloe, often described as a woman wearing a green turban, is said to haunt the plantation, and her apparition has been reported by numerous visitors over the years.

Another well-known story involves the murder of William Winter, an attorney who lived at the plantation in the 19th century. On a cold January night in 1871, Winter was shot by an unknown assailant while standing on the front porch. Mortally wounded, he staggered inside and attempted to climb the stairs to the second floor, where he collapsed and died in his wife's arms. Visitors and staff have reported hearing his dying footsteps echoing through the house, as if he is still trying to reach his beloved one last time.

In addition to these specific stories, the Myrtles Plantation is said to be haunted by the spirits of other former residents and slaves. One of the most chilling tales involves the ghost of a young girl who is often seen playing on the veranda or peering through the windows. Some believe she is the spirit of one of Woodruff's daughters, who died from the poisoning. Others think she might be one of the many children who perished on the plantation due to illness or accident.

The plantation's mirror is another source of ghostly activity. Legend has it that the mirror, which hangs in the main hallway, traps the spirits of Sara Woodruff and her children. Visitors have reported seeing handprints appear on the glass, as well as the faces of the deceased. The mirror's reflective surface is said to capture the souls of those who died tragically within the house, and it is one of the most photographed objects in the plantation.

The Myrtles Plantation also has a history of unexplained phenomena. Visitors have reported hearing strange noises, such as footsteps, whispers, and cries, even when no one else is around. Doors are said to open and close by themselves, and objects are known to move without explanation. The scent of perfume or cigar smoke sometimes lingers in the air, though no one is present to account for the smells. These occurrences have been documented by numerous paranormal investigators who have visited the site, adding to the plantation's eerie reputation.

One of the most famous ghost stories from the Myrtles Plantation involves a photograph taken by a visitor. In the picture, a shadowy figure can be seen standing near the building, even though no one was present at the time. The figure, believed by some to be the ghost of Chloe, has become one of the most iconic images associated with the plantation. The photograph has been analyzed by experts who have been unable to explain the mysterious apparition.

The plantation's reputation for being haunted has made it a popular subject for books, documentaries, and television shows. It has been featured on programs such as "Unsolved Mysteries," "Ghost Hunters," and "Most Terrifying Places in America." Each of these shows has attempted to capture evidence of the paranormal activity that is said to occur there, with varying degrees of success. The Myrtles Plantation's status as a haunted location has also drawn the attention of numerous paranormal enthusiasts and ghost hunters, many of whom have conducted their own investigations and reported their findings.

Despite the numerous stories and reported encounters, skeptics argue that many of the legends surrounding the Myrtles Plantation are based on exaggerations or fabrications. For instance, historical records show that Sara Woodruff and her children did not die from poisoning, but from yellow fever. Additionally, there is no concrete evidence to support the existence of Chloe, the supposed slave girl. Critics suggest that these tales have been embellished over time to attract tourists and enhance the plantation's mystique.

Regardless of the skepticism, the Myrtles Plantation continues to draw visitors from around the world, many of whom come with the hope of experiencing something supernatural. The plantation offers guided tours, including a "Mystery Tour" that focuses on the ghost stories and paranormal activity associated with the site. These tours provide a blend of historical facts and legends, allowing visitors to immerse themselves in the eerie atmosphere of the plantation.

In addition to the guided tours, the Myrtles Plantation also operates as a bed and breakfast, allowing guests to stay overnight in the supposedly haunted rooms. Many guests have reported strange occurrences during their stays, such as feeling an unexplained presence, hearing mysterious sounds, or seeing apparitions. These experiences often leave a lasting impression, adding to the plantation's reputation as one of the most haunted places in America.

The Myrtles Plantation's enduring legacy as a haunted house can be attributed to its rich history, the captivating stories of its past residents, and the ongoing reports of paranormal activity. Whether or not one believes in ghosts, the plantation offers a fascinating glimpse into the past and a unique opportunity to explore the intersection of history and folklore. The blend of documented history and ghostly legends creates a compelling narrative that continues to intrigue and captivate visitors.

The plantation's architecture and grounds also contribute to its haunted ambiance. The main house, with its antebellum style, wide verandas, and tall windows, evokes a sense of timelessness and grandeur. The surrounding gardens, with their moss-draped oak trees and tranquil ponds, add to the sense of mystery and otherworldliness. Walking through the property, it is easy to imagine the lives of those who lived and worked there, and to feel the lingering presence of the past.

Chapter 26: The Ghosts of Alcatraz

Alcatraz Island, located in the chilly waters of San Francisco Bay, is renowned for its historical significance as a federal prison, but it is equally famous for its chilling tales of ghosts and paranormal activities. The island's history is rich with stories of notorious criminals, desperate escape attempts, and harsh conditions, all of which have contributed to its reputation as one of the most haunted places in America. The eerie atmosphere of the abandoned prison, coupled with its dark past, creates a perfect setting for ghostly legends and mysterious occurrences that continue to captivate and terrify visitors.

Alcatraz's history as a prison began in the mid-19th century when it was first used as a military fortification and later as a military prison. However, it is its role as a federal penitentiary from 1934 to 1963 that has cemented its place in infamy. During this time, Alcatraz housed some of the most dangerous criminals in American history, including Al Capone, George "Machine Gun" Kelly, and Robert Stroud, also known as the "Birdman of Alcatraz." The prison was known for its strict rules, harsh conditions, and the inescapability of its location, surrounded by cold, treacherous waters.

The first ghost stories from Alcatraz emerged even before it became a federal prison. Native American tribes in the area believed the island to be inhabited by evil spirits, and it was used as a place of exile for members who broke tribal laws. These early tales set the stage for the island's later reputation as a haunted place. When Alcatraz was a military prison, guards and inmates reported strange sounds, eerie apparitions, and an overall feeling of unease, experiences that would only increase during its time as a federal penitentiary.

One of the most famous ghost stories from Alcatraz involves Al Capone, one of the most notorious criminals ever to be incarcerated there. Capone, who was transferred to Alcatraz in 1934, reportedly experienced haunting encounters during his time on the island. It is said that Capone, fearing for his life from fellow inmates, spent much of his time in the prison's showers, where he could be more isolated. During this time, he allegedly began to hear strange, unexplainable music emanating from the prison walls. Some accounts suggest that Capone himself played the banjo in the prison shower room to keep his sanity, but the eerie music continued even when he wasn't playing. To this day, visitors and staff have reported hearing banjo music in the shower area, despite there being no one there.

Cell 14D, one of the solitary confinement cells known as "The Hole," is another hotspot for paranormal activity. Inmates who were sent to The Hole were subjected to complete darkness and extreme isolation, often for weeks at a time. Many prisoners experienced severe psychological distress due to these harsh conditions, and several deaths were reported in these cells. One particularly chilling story involves an unnamed inmate who was placed in Cell 14D for punishment. The inmate claimed that a creature with glowing eyes was stalking him in the darkness. He screamed throughout the night, but the guards ignored his pleas. The next morning, the inmate was found dead, his face contorted in terror. While some believe he was strangled by a guard or fellow inmate, others think he was a victim of a malevolent spirit. Since then, numerous visitors have reported feeling an oppressive presence and experiencing sudden drops in temperature in Cell 14D.

The prison's former warden, James Johnston, who served during the 1930s, also reported experiencing strange phenomena. During one of his routine inspections, Johnston claimed to have heard unexplained sobbing and moaning sounds coming from within the prison walls. On another occasion, he and several guards witnessed a phantom figure dressed in 19th-century military attire walking the prison grounds. These sightings only added to the prison's haunted reputation and fueled the belief that the island was inhabited by restless spirits.

One of the most dramatic ghost stories from Alcatraz involves the infamous 1946 escape attempt known as the "Battle of Alcatraz."

During this violent confrontation, six inmates attempted a daring escape, resulting in a two-day standoff with prison guards and the U.S. Marines. In the end, two guards and three inmates were killed. The cell block where the battle took place, known as D-Block, is said to be one of the most haunted areas of the prison. Visitors and staff have reported hearing gunshots, screams, and the sounds of clanging metal doors. Some have even seen apparitions of the fallen guards and inmates, still replaying the violent events of that fateful day.

The prison hospital is another area rife with ghostly tales. During its operation, the hospital treated numerous inmates suffering from various ailments, injuries, and mental illnesses. It was also the place where several inmates died, either from natural causes or from suicides. Today, the hospital is a place of significant paranormal activity. Reports include ghostly apparitions of doctors and patients, strange lights, and the sound of disembodied voices. The most well-known ghost in the hospital is that of an inmate named Robert Stroud, the "Birdman of Alcatraz." Stroud spent 17 years in the prison hospital due to his poor health. Visitors and staff have reported seeing his apparition wandering the halls, as if still searching for his birds, which were his only companions during his imprisonment.

In addition to these specific stories, Alcatraz as a whole exudes an atmosphere of unease and foreboding. Many visitors have reported feeling an overwhelming sense of dread upon entering the prison. Some have experienced sudden chills, unexplained cold spots, and the sensation of being watched. Electronic equipment, such as cameras and audio recorders, often malfunction or capture strange anomalies when used within the prison walls. Paranormal investigators who have spent the night on the island have documented numerous instances of unexplained phenomena, including shadowy figures, disembodied voices, and objects moving on their own.

Alcatraz has also been the subject of numerous investigations by paranormal researchers and ghost hunters. Television shows like

"Ghost Adventures," "Most Haunted," and "Ghost Hunters" have all conducted investigations on the island, capturing compelling evidence of paranormal activity. During these investigations, teams have recorded unexplained sounds, captured strange images on camera, and experienced personal encounters with what they believe to be the spirits of former inmates and guards.

Despite the wealth of ghostly tales and reported encounters, skeptics argue that many of the experiences at Alcatraz can be attributed to the power of suggestion, environmental factors, and the prison's grim history. The isolation and harsh conditions experienced by inmates, combined with the violent events that took place there, could easily contribute to the eerie atmosphere and feelings of unease. Additionally, the island's cold, damp environment can create drafts and temperature fluctuations that might be mistaken for paranormal activity.

Nevertheless, the stories and experiences associated with Alcatraz continue to captivate and intrigue people from around the world. The island remains a popular tourist destination, drawing hundreds of thousands of visitors each year who are eager to explore its dark history and perhaps experience a ghostly encounter of their own. Guided tours of the prison include not only historical information but also accounts of the supernatural, allowing visitors to immerse themselves in the haunting legacy of Alcatraz.

The ghosts of Alcatraz, whether real or imagined, have become an integral part of the island's story. They serve as a reminder of the suffering and despair experienced by those who were imprisoned there and add a layer of mystery and intrigue to an already fascinating historical site. As long as people continue to be fascinated by the paranormal and the unknown, the tales of the ghosts of Alcatraz will endure, perpetuating the island's reputation as one of the most haunted places in America.

Chapter 27: The Bridgewater Triangle

The Bridgewater Triangle is an area in southeastern Massachusetts that has become infamous for its numerous reports of paranormal phenomena, ranging from sightings of strange creatures and UFOs to bizarre occurrences and unexplained disappearances. This region, encompassing approximately 200 square miles, includes several towns such as Abington, Rehoboth, Freetown, and, most notably, the town of Bridgewater, from which the triangle derives its name. It is often referred to as the "supernatural vortex" of New England due to its dense concentration of mysterious happenings.

One of the most prominent features within the Bridgewater Triangle is the Hockomock Swamp, a vast and dense wetland that is often considered the heart of the area's paranormal activity. The name "Hockomock" is derived from the Native American word meaning "place where spirits dwell," indicating that the swamp has long been regarded with fear and reverence. According to local legends, the swamp was a significant site for the Wampanoag people, who believed it to be the home of powerful spirits and deities. The swamp's eerie atmosphere and dense foliage have made it a focal point for sightings of cryptids, such as Bigfoot-like creatures and large, mysterious black cats.

In addition to cryptid sightings, the Hockomock Swamp has been a hotspot for reports of glowing orbs of light, often described as "spook lights" or "will-o'-the-wisps." These phenomena are typically seen hovering above the water or darting through the trees, creating an otherworldly spectacle that has baffled witnesses and researchers alike. Some theories suggest that these lights could be caused by swamp gases igniting spontaneously, but others believe they are manifestations of supernatural energy.

Another significant location within the Bridgewater Triangle is the Freetown-Fall River State Forest, which has a dark reputation for being the site of various sinister activities, including cult rituals and murders.

The forest's remote and dense landscape provides an ideal setting for those seeking to perform clandestine acts, and it has been linked to several high-profile criminal cases. In the late 1970s and early 1980s, the forest gained notoriety due to reports of ritualistic animal sacrifices and the discovery of mutilated animals, which some attributed to occult groups. The forest has also been the site of numerous human disappearances, adding to its ominous reputation.

The Bridgewater Triangle is not only a hotbed for cryptids and mysterious lights but also for UFO sightings. Since the 1970s, there have been numerous reports of unidentified flying objects in the area, ranging from classic disc-shaped crafts to more unconventional shapes, such as triangles and spheres. Witnesses have described these objects as moving erratically, hovering silently, and emitting bright lights that often change color. Some researchers have suggested that the region's geological features, such as its high concentration of quartz and granite, might create an electromagnetic field that attracts or amplifies UFO activity.

One of the most famous UFO sightings in the Bridgewater Triangle occurred in 1979 when a local man named William Russo encountered a strange, glowing object while walking his dog late at night. Russo described the object as being about the size of a car and emitting a pulsating blue light. As he watched, the object hovered silently above the ground before suddenly accelerating and disappearing into the night sky. Russo's account was later corroborated by other witnesses who reported seeing similar objects in the area around the same time.

In addition to UFO sightings, the Bridgewater Triangle has a long history of ghostly encounters and haunted locations. One of the most well-known haunted sites is the Bridgewater State Hospital, a psychiatric facility that has been the subject of numerous ghost stories and paranormal investigations. Visitors and staff have reported hearing disembodied voices, footsteps, and even seeing apparitions of former patients who died under mysterious or tragic circumstances. The hospital's unsettling history and reputation for mistreatment of patients have only fueled the tales of lingering spirits.

Another haunted location within the triangle is the Taunton State Hospital, another psychiatric facility with a similarly dark past. Established in the 19th century, the hospital has been the site of countless reports of paranormal activity, including sightings of shadowy figures, unexplained cold spots, and objects moving on their own. The hospital's old, dilapidated buildings and eerie atmosphere have made it a popular destination for ghost hunters and paranormal enthusiasts.

In addition to these well-known sites, many private homes and businesses within the Bridgewater Triangle have been reported to be haunted. Residents have recounted stories of hearing strange noises, seeing apparitions, and experiencing other unexplained phenomena. Some believe that the area's long and tumultuous history, including violent conflicts between Native American tribes and European settlers, has left a lingering spiritual presence that contributes to the region's high level of paranormal activity.

Despite the numerous reports and investigations, the true nature of the Bridgewater Triangle remains a mystery. Skeptics argue that the stories of paranormal activity are the result of folklore, psychological suggestion, and natural phenomena being misinterpreted as supernatural. However, the sheer volume and consistency of the reports suggest that there may be more to the region's mysteries than simple superstition. Some researchers have proposed that the Bridgewater Triangle could be an example of a "window area," a place where the boundaries between different dimensions or realities are thinner, allowing for an increased likelihood of encounters with the paranormal.

The Bridgewater Triangle continues to captivate the imagination of both locals and visitors, drawing in those who are curious about the unknown and eager to experience its mysteries firsthand. The region has been the subject of numerous books, documentaries, and television shows, further cementing its status as one of the most enigmatic and intriguing paranormal hotspots in the United States. Whether one believes in the supernatural or not, there is no denying that the Bridgewater Triangle has a unique and compelling allure that continues to inspire fascination and wonder.

Chapter 28: The Hinterkaifeck Murders

The Hinterkaifeck Murders, one of the most enigmatic and gruesome unsolved crimes in German history, occurred on a remote farmstead in Bavaria in 1922. The farm, known as Hinterkaifeck, was situated between the towns of Ingolstadt and Schrobenhausen, approximately 70 kilometers north of Munich. This case has fascinated and perplexed investigators, historians, and true crime enthusiasts for over a century, not only because of the brutal nature of the murders but also due to the bizarre and unsettling circumstances surrounding the crime.

The story of Hinterkaifeck begins with the Gruber family, who resided on the farmstead. The family consisted of Andreas Gruber, a 63-year-old patriarch known for his strict and sometimes abusive demeanor; his 72-year-old wife, Cäzilia; their widowed daughter, Viktoria Gabriel, aged 35; and Viktoria's two children, 7-year-old Cäzilia and 2-year-old Josef. The farm also employed a maid, Maria Baumgartner, who had only recently started working there, replacing the previous maid who had abruptly left her position, allegedly citing fears of the property being haunted.

In the days leading up to the murders, Andreas Gruber reported hearing strange noises in the attic and finding unexplained footprints in the snow leading to the farmhouse but none leading away. He also mentioned that several items had gone missing or been moved around the property without explanation. Despite these ominous signs, the family remained on the farm, seemingly unaware of the impending tragedy.

On the night of March 31, 1922, something horrifying happened at Hinterkaifeck. Over the next few days, neighbors began to notice the family's absence. Their mail accumulated at the local post office, and young Cäzilia failed to attend school. Concerned by the family's uncharacteristic silence, neighbors visited the farm on April 4. What they discovered was a scene of unimaginable horror.

The bodies of Andreas, Cäzilia, Viktoria, and young Cäzilia were found in the barn, gruesomely murdered with a mattock, a farming tool resembling a pickaxe. It appeared that they had been lured one by one into the barn, where they were then killed. The two-year-old Josef and the maid Maria were found inside the house, having also been brutally slain. The entire family had suffered severe head wounds, indicating that the murders were carried out with extreme violence.

Investigators were immediately puzzled by several aspects of the case. Despite the brutal nature of the crime, the perpetrator or perpetrators seemed to have stayed on the farm for several days after the murders. Evidence suggested that they had fed the livestock, eaten the family's food, and even lit fires in the hearths. This chilling behavior indicated a level of familiarity with the farm and its routines, raising the possibility that the killer was someone known to the family or, at the very least, someone who had observed them closely.

Adding to the mystery were the strange occurrences leading up to the murders. The previous maid's departure, citing fears of hauntings, took on a more sinister tone in retrospect. Andreas Gruber's discovery of footprints in the snow and unexplained disturbances around the property suggested that someone had been spying on the family and possibly living on or near the farm for an extended period before the murders.

The investigation into the Hinterkaifeck Murders was extensive, but despite numerous suspects and theories, no definitive conclusion was reached. Several individuals were questioned, including local residents and even distant relatives of the Gruber family, but no arrests were made. One theory that gained traction was that Viktoria's son Josef was the product of an incestuous relationship between her and her father, Andreas. This theory posited that someone close to the family, possibly Viktoria's husband or another relative, might have killed them in a fit of rage or to hide the shame of the incest. However, this theory, like many others, remained speculative.

Over the years, numerous other theories have been proposed. Some suggested that the murders were the result of a botched robbery, but this was largely discounted due to the fact that large sums of money were found untouched in the house. Others believed that the murders were committed by a vagrant or a transient worker familiar with the farm. The lack of any clear motive or suspects has led to widespread speculation and a variety of theories, but none have provided a satisfactory explanation for the horrific events at Hinterkaifeck.

The mystery of the Hinterkaifeck Murders has only deepened over time. In the decades following the crime, several investigators and journalists have attempted to solve the case, but all have come up short. The farmhouse was eventually demolished in 1923, a year after the murders, but the case continued to haunt the local community. In 2007, a group of forensic students from the Police Academy in Fürstenfeldbruck used modern criminal profiling techniques to re-examine the case. While they identified a prime suspect based on available evidence, they declined to publicly name the individual, citing the lack of concrete proof and the fact that the suspect was long deceased.

The Hinterkaifeck Murders remain one of Germany's most chilling unsolved mysteries. The combination of the brutal killings, the eerie prelude involving strange noises and sightings, and the unsettling post-murder behavior of the perpetrator or perpetrators creates a haunting narrative that has captivated imaginations worldwide. The case highlights the dark and often inexplicable side of human nature, reminding us that some mysteries, no matter how much time passes or how much technology advances, may never be fully understood or solved.

Chapter 29: The Ghostly Hitchhiker of Blue Bell Hill

The legend of the Ghostly Hitchhiker of Blue Bell Hill is one of the most enduring and chilling tales in British folklore, capturing the imaginations of locals and paranormal enthusiasts alike. Situated near Maidstone in Kent, Blue Bell Hill is a seemingly innocuous stretch of the A229 road. However, it has become infamous for its numerous reports of ghostly apparitions, particularly that of a spectral hitchhiker who is said to haunt the area. The story of the Ghostly Hitchhiker is steeped in mystery and has been recounted in various forms for decades, contributing to its status as a modern urban legend.

The origins of the Blue Bell Hill ghost story are often traced back to a tragic event that occurred on November 19, 1965. On that day, a young bride-to-be named Suzanne Browne, along with two of her friends, Patricia Ferguson and Judith Langham, were involved in a horrific car accident while traveling along Blue Bell Hill. Suzanne was due to be married the next day, but the car she was in collided head-on with another vehicle, resulting in fatal injuries. Suzanne and Patricia died at the scene, while Judith succumbed to her injuries five days later. This tragic accident has often been linked to the subsequent sightings of a ghostly figure on the hill.

The most common version of the Ghostly Hitchhiker story involves motorists traveling along the A229 who encounter a young woman, often described as wearing a white dress or wedding gown, standing by the roadside and attempting to flag down a ride. Those who stop to assist her are usually given a location nearby to which she needs to be taken. However, during the journey, she either vanishes from the vehicle or, upon arriving at the destination, disappears into thin air. In some accounts, the ghostly figure is seen only in the rearview mirror, causing drivers to panic and veer off the road.

One of the most famous sightings occurred in November 1974, when a man named Maurice Goodenough reported picking up a distressed young woman on Blue Bell Hill. He described her as wearing a light-colored coat and appearing visibly shaken. He offered her a ride, and she requested to be taken to Chatham, a nearby town. During the journey, she reportedly vanished from the car without a trace. Goodenough, deeply disturbed by the encounter, reported the incident to the police. A subsequent investigation revealed no signs of the woman he described, and the case was eventually closed as an unexplained mystery.

In another well-documented case from 1992, a motorist named Ian Sharpe reported hitting a young woman who suddenly appeared in front of his car on Blue Bell Hill. Believing he had struck a pedestrian; Sharpe stopped and searched the area but found no sign of the woman or any evidence of an accident. When he contacted the police, they conducted a thorough investigation but found no clues. Sharpe's account was eerily similar to other reports from drivers who had experienced the same phenomenon on the same stretch of road.

The Ghostly Hitchhiker legend has evolved over the years, with various iterations adding to its mystique. Some versions of the story describe the apparition as a bride-to-be, possibly linking her to Suzanne Browne and the tragic events of 1965. Other accounts suggest that the ghost is a different woman altogether, possibly another victim of a road accident or someone who met a violent end in the area. The common thread in these stories is the spectral figure's sudden appearance and equally sudden disappearance, leaving witnesses shaken and often questioning their sanity.

The haunted reputation of Blue Bell Hill has attracted numerous paranormal investigators and enthusiasts, all eager to uncover the truth behind the ghostly sightings. Some have speculated that the area might be a "thin place," where the boundaries between the physical world and the spiritual realm are less distinct, allowing for such supernatural encounters. Others suggest that the ghostly hitchhiker is a form of residual haunting, where a traumatic event has left an imprint on the environment, causing the same scene to replay itself repeatedly.

Skeptics, on the other hand, argue that the sightings can be attributed to psychological factors, such as the power of suggestion, hallucinations, or the misinterpretation of natural phenomena. The eerie atmosphere of Blue Bell Hill, particularly at night, could also play a role in creating a sense of unease and heightening the likelihood of witnessing something out of the ordinary. The presence of fog, shadows, and the interplay of light from passing cars might contribute to the illusion of a ghostly figure.

Despite the skepticism, the legend of the Ghostly Hitchhiker persists, fueled by a steady stream of reports and personal testimonies. Over the years, several books, documentaries, and television programs have explored the phenomenon, further cementing its place in local lore. Each new account adds a layer of intrigue to the story, keeping the mystery alive and ensuring that Blue Bell Hill remains a focal point for those interested in the paranormal.

Interestingly, the tale of the ghostly hitchhiker is not unique to Blue Bell Hill but is part of a broader folklore motif known as the "vanishing hitchhiker." Similar stories exist in various cultures around the world, often involving a traveler who encounters a mysterious figure seeking a ride, only for the figure to disappear under inexplicable circumstances. These tales typically share common themes of tragedy, loss, and the thin line between life and death, suggesting a universal human fascination with the unknown and the afterlife.

Chapter 30: The Shadow People Phenomenon

The phenomenon of Shadow People is a deeply intriguing and unsettling aspect of the paranormal world, sparking interest and fear across cultures and societies. Shadow People are described as dark, shadowy figures that appear to have a human-like form but lack distinct features. They are often reported to be seen out of the corner of one's eye or fleetingly in dark or dimly lit areas. The phenomenon has been the subject of numerous accounts and reports, with experiences ranging from mere curiosity to intense fear and dread. The mystery of Shadow People has given rise to a wide array of theories and interpretations, each attempting to explain who or what these entities might be and why they appear to us.

One of the most common descriptions of Shadow People is that of a tall, dark silhouette, often perceived as male, with no discernible facial features or clothing. Some reports suggest that these figures wear a hat, leading to the term "Hat Man" being used to describe such encounters. Despite their lack of distinct characteristics, Shadow People are often perceived as exuding a sense of menace or malevolence. Witnesses frequently describe a feeling of being watched or a sense of impending doom when encountering these entities. Some even report feeling paralyzed with fear or experiencing a sudden drop in temperature when in the presence of a Shadow Person.

The origins of the Shadow People phenomenon are difficult to pinpoint, but stories and legends of shadowy figures have been present in various cultures for centuries. In many indigenous cultures, shadowy figures are often seen as spirits or manifestations of ancestors, while in others, they are regarded as malevolent entities or omens of doom. The widespread nature of these accounts suggests that Shadow People, or beings like them, are a part of the human experience and have been for a very long time.

One of the earliest mentions of shadowy beings in Western culture can be found in the work of German psychiatrist Dr. Johann Christian Reil in the early 19th century. Reil's studies included descriptions of patients who reported seeing dark, shadowy figures that seemed to follow or observe them. However, it wasn't until the late 20th century that the term "Shadow People" began to gain prominence, largely due to the rise of paranormal investigations and the increased sharing of personal experiences through media such as radio shows, books, and, more recently, the internet.

There are several theories that attempt to explain the Shadow People phenomenon, ranging from the psychological to the supernatural. One of the most widely accepted scientific explanations is that Shadow People are a product of our brains misinterpreting visual stimuli, particularly in low-light conditions. This phenomenon is known as pareidolia, where the brain tends to perceive familiar shapes or figures, such as human forms, in random patterns or shadows. This can happen more frequently when we are tired, stressed, or in a heightened state of awareness, leading to a greater likelihood of interpreting vague stimuli as something sinister.

Another psychological explanation suggests that Shadow People might be a manifestation of sleep paralysis, a condition where an individual is temporarily unable to move or speak while falling asleep or waking up. During sleep paralysis, people often experience hallucinations, including seeing shadowy figures, which can feel incredibly real and frightening. These experiences are usually accompanied by a sense of pressure on the chest, making it difficult to breathe, and a feeling of being watched or threatened.

Some researchers propose that Shadow People could be a type of hallucination brought on by certain neurological conditions or the use of substances that alter brain chemistry. For example, people with schizophrenia or those experiencing high levels of stress or anxiety may be more prone to seeing shadowy figures. Additionally, the use of drugs such as LSD or other hallucinogens can induce visions of dark, shadowy beings. This theory suggests that Shadow People might be a byproduct of altered states of consciousness, whether through illness, stress, or substance use.

Despite these scientific explanations, many people believe that Shadow People are not merely a product of the mind but represent something more supernatural or otherworldly. Some theories suggest that they are ghosts or spirits, lingering in the human world due to unfinished business or a traumatic death. In this view, Shadow People are thought to be souls trapped between worlds, unable to move on to the afterlife and manifesting as shadowy figures as a result.

Another popular supernatural theory posits that Shadow People are interdimensional beings, entities that exist in a parallel dimension but occasionally intersect with our own. This idea is often supported by reports of Shadow People appearing suddenly and disappearing just as quickly, as if moving between dimensions. Some proponents of this theory believe that Shadow People might be able to travel between worlds at will, perhaps observing or interacting with our reality for purposes unknown to us.

A darker interpretation suggests that Shadow People are demonic entities, feeding off the fear and negative emotions of those who encounter them. In this view, Shadow People are seen as malevolent forces, intent on causing harm or instilling terror in their victims. Reports of Shadow People accompanied by a sense of dread, unease, or malevolent intent lend credence to this theory. Some people who have experienced encounters with Shadow People describe feeling an overwhelming sense of evil or danger, leading them to believe that these entities are not benign but have sinister motives.

There are also those who believe that Shadow People are the spirits of the dead who have not found peace. According to this theory, these entities are the souls of individuals who died suddenly or violently, and as a result, their spirits remain earthbound. Unable to find rest, they appear as shadowy figures, perhaps seeking resolution or recognition from the living. This interpretation often ties in with cultural beliefs about restless spirits and the need for rituals or ceremonies to help them move on.

Despite the various theories and explanations, the experiences of those who have encountered Shadow People remain deeply personal and often unsettling. Many individuals report seeing these figures in their homes, typically in bedrooms or hallways, where they feel most vulnerable. Some describe waking up to find a shadowy figure standing at the foot of their bed or lurking in a corner, watching them. Others recount experiences of seeing Shadow People while walking alone at night or in isolated areas, where the sudden appearance of a dark, human-like shape can be particularly frightening.

The impact of these encounters can be profound, leaving individuals with lasting feelings of fear, anxiety, or curiosity about the nature of their experience. Some people become obsessed with finding answers or explanations, while others seek help from paranormal investigators, spiritual advisors, or mental health professionals to understand and cope with their experiences.

The phenomenon of Shadow People has also permeated popular culture, appearing in books, movies, and television shows. These depictions often emphasize the mysterious and malevolent aspects of Shadow People, reinforcing their reputation as ominous and frightening entities. In many fictional portrayals, Shadow People are shown as sinister beings, capable of causing harm or even possessing those they encounter. These representations have helped to shape public perception of Shadow People, contributing to their status as one of the most unsettling elements of the paranormal world.

Chapter 31: The Black-Eyed Children

The phenomenon of Black-Eyed Children is one of the more recent additions to the world of paranormal legends, yet it has quickly become one of the most disturbing and enigmatic. Reports of these eerie entities began to emerge in the late 20th century and have since proliferated across various platforms, including online forums, radio shows, and books dedicated to the paranormal. Black-Eyed Children are typically described as having pale skin, monotone voices, and most strikingly, completely black eyes devoid of any white sclera or iris. They are usually reported to be between the ages of six and sixteen and are often seen wearing outdated or unusual clothing. These children are known for their unnerving behavior, as they often approach adults at their homes or cars, asking for assistance or entry. The sheer eeriness of these encounters has made Black-Eyed Children a subject of intense fascination and fear, with numerous theories attempting to explain their origin and purpose.

The legend of the Black-Eyed Children first gained widespread attention in the late 1990s, largely thanks to a now-famous post by journalist Brian Bethel on a paranormal message board in 1996. Bethel recounted a terrifying encounter he had with two Black-Eyed Children in Abilene, Texas. According to his account, he was sitting in his car in a parking lot, preparing to pay a bill at a nearby drop box, when two boys, estimated to be around nine to twelve years old, approached his vehicle. They knocked on his window and asked for a ride to their home to get money for a movie they wanted to see. Bethel described feeling an overwhelming sense of fear and unease, despite the boys' polite request. It was only when he looked more closely at their faces that he noticed their eyes were completely black. Panicked, he refused their request and quickly drove away, leaving the boys behind.

Bethel's story quickly went viral, spreading across the internet and leading to a surge in similar reports from people all over the world.

Many of these accounts share common elements: the Black-Eyed Children typically appear at night, often in isolated or suburban areas. They usually travel in pairs and approach their target with a request, such as needing to use the phone, wanting a ride, or asking for something to eat or drink. Despite their outwardly polite demeanor, these children seem to emanate an inexplicable aura of fear and dread, causing those who encounter them to feel a strong instinct to flee or avoid interaction.

One of the most unsettling aspects of these encounters is the insistence of the Black-Eyed Children on being allowed inside the target's home or car. They often repeat their request multiple times, sometimes even growing more insistent or aggressive when denied. This behavior has led to speculation that they require an invitation to enter, much like the mythical vampire. Some theorists suggest that granting them entry could lead to dire consequences, although there are few reports of what actually happens if they are allowed inside, as most witnesses report feeling an overwhelming sense of danger and refuse to let them in.

The black eyes of these children are perhaps their most disturbing feature and are consistently reported across multiple accounts. Unlike other features, which might vary slightly between reports, the black eyes are a constant and defining characteristic. The total absence of sclera or iris gives the impression of hollow, soulless pits, contributing significantly to the fear and unease experienced by witnesses. Some speculate that the black eyes might be a sign of possession or otherworldly origin, indicating that these beings are not human or are under the influence of some malevolent force.

There are several theories regarding the nature and origin of the Black-Eyed Children, each attempting to explain the eerie and unexplainable aspects of these encounters. One popular theory is that they are extraterrestrial beings, possibly hybrids or genetically engineered by aliens. This theory suggests that the black eyes could be indicative of their alien nature, similar to the large, dark eyes commonly attributed to the "grey" aliens in UFO lore. Proponents of this theory point to the children's unusual behavior, outdated clothing, and lack of knowledge about modern customs as evidence that they are not from this world.

Another theory posits that the Black-Eyed Children are demonic entities or manifestations of evil spirits. According to this view, the children might be trying to gain entry to a person's home or car to cause harm or possess them. The black eyes are seen as a sign of their malevolent nature, and the intense fear they provoke is thought to be a result of their evil aura. Some religious or spiritual interpretations suggest that these entities are trying to harvest human souls or are part of a larger demonic agenda.

A third theory suggests that the Black-Eyed Children could be a form of urban legend or mass hysteria, fueled by the power of suggestion and the spread of stories through modern media. According to this perspective, the widespread nature of these reports can be attributed to psychological factors, such as pareidolia, where the mind perceives patterns or familiar shapes, and the influence of cultural narratives about supernatural beings. The shared characteristics of the reports might be a result of people subconsciously embellishing their experiences to fit the template of the Black-Eyed Children legend.

Some researchers believe that the phenomenon could be a combination of several factors, including genuine encounters with unknown entities and the influence of folklore and mass media. They suggest that the Black-Eyed Children could be an example of a modern myth that has evolved in response to the anxieties and uncertainties of contemporary life. The stories about these children tap into deep-seated fears about strangers, the unknown, and the loss of control, making them a powerful and resonant legend.

Despite the many theories and explanations, there is no concrete evidence to definitively prove the existence or nature of the Black-Eyed

Children. Most reports are anecdotal, and there is a lack of physical evidence or verifiable documentation. However, the consistency of the accounts and the genuine fear expressed by those who have encountered these entities suggest that there is something more to the phenomenon than mere fiction or imagination.

In addition to the numerous individual reports, the legend of the Black-Eyed Children has inspired a range of cultural responses, including books, movies, and television shows. These portrayals often emphasize the sinister and supernatural aspects of the phenomenon, depicting the children as malevolent beings with dark and dangerous intentions. These media representations have helped to cement the image of the Black-Eyed Children as one of the most chilling figures in modern paranormal lore.

The enduring appeal of the Black-Eyed Children legend can be attributed to several factors. First, the simplicity and clarity of the story make it easy to retell and spread, allowing it to reach a wide audience. The image of a child with black, soulless eyes is inherently unsettling and taps into primal fears about the unknown and the loss of safety. Additionally, the lack of a definitive explanation for the phenomenon leaves room for endless speculation and debate, keeping the legend alive and relevant.

The Black-Eyed Children phenomenon also reflects broader cultural anxieties and concerns. The idea of children, typically seen as symbols of innocence and vulnerability, being transformed into malevolent or otherworldly beings can be interpreted as a metaphor for the loss of innocence or the corruption of purity in a complex and dangerous world. The insistence of the Black-Eyed Children on being let inside might symbolize fears about the infiltration of evil or the loss of personal control and safety.

Chapter 32: The Phantom of the Opera House

The legend of the Phantom of the Opera House is one of the most captivating and enduring tales in the realm of the supernatural and gothic literature. Its origins can be traced back to the late 19th century, specifically to Gaston Leroux's novel "Le Fantôme de l'Opéra," published in 1910. The story has since become a cultural phenomenon, inspiring countless adaptations in film, theater, and other media. It centers on the mysterious and tragic figure of the Phantom, a disfigured musical genius who haunts the Paris Opera House. The legend blends elements of horror, romance, and tragedy, creating a rich and multilayered narrative that continues to captivate audiences around the world.

Gaston Leroux's "The Phantom of the Opera" is set in the opulent and labyrinthine Paris Opera House, officially known as the Palais Garnier. The novel introduces us to a series of strange and inexplicable events that suggest the presence of a ghostly figure haunting the opera house. The story begins with the opera house managers, Monsieur Debienne and Monsieur Poligny, who are retiring and handing over their duties to their successors, Armand Moncharmin and Firmin Richard. They warn the new managers about the Phantom, describing him as a spectral presence who demands a private box at all performances and a monthly salary of 20,000 francs. Although skeptical at first, Moncharmin and Richard soon experience the Phantom's wrath firsthand, as strange accidents and unexplained phenomena begin to plague the opera house.

The central figure of the novel is Erik, the Phantom, a man born with a grotesque facial deformity that has led him to live a life of isolation and despair. He was once a brilliant architect and musician, but his appearance forced him to retreat to the underground catacombs of the opera house, where he constructs a hidden lair. Erik is a complex character, a blend of villain and victim, whose genius is matched only by his deep sense of loneliness and longing for acceptance. His love for Christine Daaé, a beautiful and talented young singer, drives the narrative and adds layers of both horror and pathos to the story.

Christine Daaé, the novel's heroine, is an orphan who was raised by her father, a renowned Swedish violinist. Before his death, her father told her stories of an "Angel of Music" who would guide and protect her. After his death, Christine finds herself drawn to the Paris Opera House, where she begins her career in the chorus. Her beauty and talent soon attract the attention of Erik, who becomes infatuated with her. Believing him to be the Angel of Music her father had promised, Christine allows herself to be tutored by Erik, who teaches her to sing with an otherworldly skill. However, she soon discovers the true nature of her mysterious benefactor and is horrified by his appearance and obsession with her.

The relationship between Christine and Erik is fraught with tension and complexity. On the one hand, Erik is a mentor and a father figure, guiding Christine's musical development and helping her achieve her dreams. On the other hand, his love for her is possessive and obsessive, driven by a desire for control and a deep-seated fear of rejection. Christine, meanwhile, is torn between gratitude and fear, caught in a web of emotions that ultimately leads her to confront the dark and tragic figure of the Phantom.

Raoul de Chagny, a childhood friend of Christine and her romantic interest, plays a crucial role in the story. As a wealthy and handsome young nobleman, Raoul represents a world of light and normalcy, in stark contrast to the dark and twisted existence of the Phantom. Raoul's love for Christine is pure and selfless, and he is determined to rescue her from the clutches of the Phantom. This love triangle between Christine, Erik, and Raoul adds an element of romantic tension to the story, heightening the stakes and underscoring the themes of love, obsession, and sacrifice.

The climax of the novel occurs when Erik, desperate to possess Christine, kidnaps her and takes her to his underground lair. He gives her an ultimatum: she must choose to stay with him forever or he will destroy the opera house, killing everyone inside. In a dramatic and heart-wrenching scene, Christine agrees to stay with Erik in order to save the lives of those in the opera house. Touched by her selflessness and moved by her compassion, Erik ultimately releases her and allows her to leave with Raoul. He then retreats to his lair, where he is believed to have died of a broken heart.

The enduring appeal of "The Phantom of the Opera" lies in its rich and multilayered narrative, which combines elements of horror, romance, and tragedy. The story explores themes of love and obsession, beauty and monstrosity, and the tension between light and darkness. The character of Erik, in particular, is a fascinating study in duality, embodying both the monstrous and the pitiable, the genius and the outcast. His tragic fate underscores the novel's exploration of the human condition, the longing for connection, and the pain of rejection and isolation.

The novel's setting, the Paris Opera House, plays a crucial role in creating the atmosphere of mystery and gothic horror that pervades the story. The opera house, with its grand architecture, hidden passageways, and labyrinthine catacombs, serves as a physical manifestation of the novel's themes of beauty and darkness, art and madness. The setting adds a layer of authenticity and historical richness to the narrative, grounding the fantastical elements of the story in a real and tangible location.

"The Phantom of the Opera" has inspired countless adaptations in various media, each adding its own interpretation and twist to the original story. The most famous of these is Andrew Lloyd Webber's 1986 musical, which has become one of the longest-running shows in Broadway history. The musical, with its haunting score and lavish production, has brought the story of the Phantom to a global audience, cementing its place in popular culture. Other notable adaptations include the 1925 silent film starring Lon Chaney, the 2004 film directed by Joel Schumacher, and numerous television, radio, and literary adaptations.

The legend of the Phantom has also sparked a range of cultural responses and interpretations. Some view the Phantom as a symbol of the misunderstood artist, driven to madness by society's rejection and cruelty. Others see him as a cautionary figure, representing the dangers of unchecked obsession and the destructive power of unrequited love. The story has also been interpreted as a critique of the superficiality of beauty and the ways in which society marginalizes those who do not conform to its standards.

In addition to its cultural impact, the story of the Phantom has also given rise to numerous urban legends and ghost stories associated with the Paris Opera House. It is said that the opera house is haunted by the ghost of a man who was killed during the construction of the building, and that strange and inexplicable events continue to occur there to this day. These stories, while likely apocryphal, add an extra layer of intrigue and mystique to the already captivating legend of the Phantom.

The enduring popularity of "The Phantom of the Opera" can be attributed to its timeless themes, complex characters, and the universal appeal of its narrative. The story resonates with audiences on multiple levels, offering a thrilling and emotionally rich experience that transcends time and cultural boundaries. Whether viewed as a gothic horror, a tragic love story, or a commentary on the human condition, the legend of the Phantom continues to captivate and inspire, ensuring its place as one of the most beloved and enduring tales in the realm of literature and popular culture.

Chapter 33: The Ghosts of Gettysburg

The Ghosts of Gettysburg form a haunting narrative that intertwines the historical significance of one of the bloodiest battles of the American Civil War with a rich tapestry of paranormal lore. The Battle of Gettysburg, which took place from July 1 to July 3, 1863, was a pivotal moment in the war, resulting in a Union victory that turned the tide against the Confederates. However, the victory came at a tremendous cost, with over 50,000 soldiers killed, wounded, or missing. The immense loss of life and the intense emotional and physical trauma experienced by those who fought have left an indelible mark on the landscape of Gettysburg, which many believe has given rise to a myriad of ghostly phenomena. The town of Gettysburg, Pennsylvania, and its surrounding areas are reputed to be among the most haunted locations in the United States, with numerous reports of apparitions, strange sounds, and unexplained occurrences that have fascinated and frightened both locals and visitors for generations.

The story of the Gettysburg ghosts begins with the battle itself, a brutal and chaotic conflict that saw the fields and hillsides around the town transformed into a scene of unimaginable carnage. The battle involved more than 160,000 soldiers and resulted in a staggering number of casualties. The fields were littered with the bodies of the dead and dying, and the cries of the wounded filled the air. The horror of the battle was compounded by the intense heat of the summer sun, the stench of death, and the overwhelming sense of despair and desperation. It is said that the sheer scale of suffering and loss experienced at Gettysburg has left a lingering energy that continues to manifest in the form of ghostly phenomena.

One of the most famous haunted locations in Gettysburg is the Gettysburg National Military Park, which encompasses many of the key sites of the battle, including Cemetery Hill, Devil's Den, Little Round Top, and the fields where Pickett's Charge took place. Visitors to the park often report seeing ghostly soldiers, hearing the sounds of battle, and experiencing an eerie sense of being watched or followed. One of the most commonly reported phenomena is the sight of spectral figures in Civil War uniforms, wandering the fields and forests as if still searching for their comrades or reliving their final moments. These apparitions are often seen in the early morning or late evening, when the light is dim and the atmosphere is thick with the weight of history.

Cemetery Hill, a key position during the battle and the site of some of the fiercest fighting, is one of the most haunted locations in Gettysburg. Visitors to the hill have reported seeing ghostly soldiers standing guard, hearing the sounds of cannon fire and musket shots, and experiencing a sense of unease and sadness. The hill is also home to Evergreen Cemetery, where many soldiers who died in the battle are buried. The cemetery is said to be haunted by the spirits of these fallen soldiers, who are seen wandering among the graves or standing silently beside their final resting places.

Devil's Den, a rocky outcrop that was the scene of intense fighting on the second day of the battle, is another site with a reputation for paranormal activity. The area is known for its eerie atmosphere and reports of ghostly apparitions, including a mysterious figure known as the "Devil's Den Soldier." This ghost is often described as a barefoot man in a tattered Confederate uniform, who appears and disappears among the rocks. Visitors have also reported hearing the sounds of phantom gunfire and the cries of the wounded, as well as experiencing sudden drops in temperature and an overwhelming sense of dread.

Little Round Top, a strategic hill that was the site of a critical Union defense, is also said to be haunted by the ghosts of soldiers who fought and died there. One of the most famous stories involves the ghost of a Union soldier who is often seen standing on the hill, gazing out over the battlefield. This apparition is believed to be the spirit of Colonel Joshua Chamberlain, who led the 20th Maine regiment in a desperate and successful defense of the hill. Visitors to Little Round Top have also reported hearing the sounds of battle, feeling cold spots, and seeing ghostly figures moving through the trees and underbrush.

The fields where Pickett's Charge took place are another area of intense paranormal activity. This final and doomed assault by Confederate forces resulted in devastating losses and is often described as the high-water mark of the Confederacy. The fields are said to be haunted by the ghosts of the soldiers who fell there, with many reports of ghostly figures seen marching across the fields or standing silently in the distance. Visitors have also reported hearing the sounds of battle, including the roar of cannon fire and the cries of the wounded, as well as experiencing a sense of overwhelming sadness and despair.

The town of Gettysburg itself is also reputed to be haunted, with numerous buildings and locations associated with ghostly phenomena. The Gettysburg Hotel, located in the center of town, is said to be haunted by the ghost of a woman named Rachel, who died in a fire in the late 1800s. Guests at the hotel have reported seeing her apparition, hearing strange noises, and experiencing unexplained cold spots. Another haunted location is the Jennie Wade House, where Jennie Wade, the only civilian killed during the battle, was struck by a stray bullet while kneading dough in her sister's kitchen. Her ghost is said to haunt the house, and visitors have reported seeing her apparition, hearing strange noises, and feeling a sense of sadness and unease.

The Farnsworth House Inn, another historic building in Gettysburg, is also known for its paranormal activity. The inn served as a Confederate hospital during the battle, and it is said to be haunted by the ghosts of soldiers who died there. Guests have reported hearing footsteps, seeing ghostly figures, and experiencing other unexplained phenomena. The inn offers ghost tours and paranormal investigations, and it has become a popular destination for those interested in the supernatural.

One of the most famous ghost stories associated with Gettysburg involves the ghost of General Robert E. Lee. According to legend, Lee's ghost has been seen on the battlefield, particularly in the area where Pickett's Charge took place. Witnesses have reported seeing a spectral figure in a Confederate uniform, riding a horse and gazing out over the battlefield. This apparition is believed to be the spirit of Lee, still mourning the loss of his men and the failure of his assault.

Another well-known ghost story involves the spirit of a soldier known as the "Sarge." This ghost is often seen in the basement of the Soldiers' National Museum, which served as a field hospital during the battle. The Sarge is described as a tall, imposing figure in a Union uniform, who is often seen standing silently or pacing the basement. Visitors to the museum have reported feeling a sense of unease and hearing strange noises, including the sound of footsteps and the moaning of the wounded.

The ghost of a Confederate soldier named "Charlie" is also said to haunt the basement of the Farnsworth House Inn. According to legend, Charlie was a sharpshooter who was killed during the battle, and his spirit has remained in the inn ever since. Guests and staff at the inn have reported seeing Charlie's ghost, hearing strange noises, and experiencing unexplained cold spots. The inn has become a popular destination for ghost hunters and paranormal enthusiasts, who come to investigate the reports of ghostly activity.

The battlefield itself is also known for its paranormal phenomena, with many reports of ghostly soldiers, strange lights, and unexplained sounds. Visitors to the battlefield have reported seeing spectral figures in Civil War uniforms, hearing the sounds of battle, and feeling an eerie sense of being watched. One of the most famous stories involves the ghost of a Confederate soldier who is often seen standing guard at the entrance to the battlefield, saluting visitors as they pass by. This apparition is believed to be the spirit of a soldier who died during the battle and remains on duty, even in death.

The Ghosts of Gettysburg have become a significant part of the town's identity and a major draw for tourists and paranormal enthusiasts. The town offers a variety of ghost tours, paranormal investigations, and other activities that allow visitors to explore the haunted history of Gettysburg. These tours often include visits to the most haunted locations in the town and the battlefield, where guides share stories of ghostly encounters and the history of the battle. The popularity of these tours has helped to keep the legend of the Gettysburg ghosts alive and has contributed to the town's reputation as one of the most haunted places in the United States.

The phenomenon of the Ghosts of Gettysburg also raises interesting questions about the nature of ghosts and the relationship between history and the paranormal. Some researchers believe that the intense emotional energy and trauma experienced during the battle may have created a kind of "psychic imprint" on the landscape, which continues to manifest as ghostly phenomena. Others suggest that the ghosts of Gettysburg may be the spirits of soldiers who are unable or unwilling to move on, still bound to the place where they fought and died.

The Gettysburg ghosts also serve as a powerful reminder of the human cost of war and the enduring impact of historical events. The stories of ghostly soldiers and haunted locations provide a tangible connection to the past, allowing us to remember and honor the sacrifices of those who fought and died at Gettysburg. The ghosts of Gettysburg are not just a source of fear and fascination, but also a poignant reminder of the history and legacy of the Civil War.

Chapter 34: The Beast of Gévaudan

The tale of the Beast of Gévaudan is a chilling and enigmatic chapter in the annals of French history, weaving together elements of terror, mystery, and folklore. Between 1764 and 1767, a series of brutal attacks by a mysterious creature terrorized the region of Gévaudan in the former province of Languedoc, now part of modern-day Lozère and Haute-Loire in south-central France. These attacks left a profound mark on the collective psyche of the inhabitants and sparked widespread panic across the nation. The Beast of Gévaudan is a subject of enduring fascination, not only for its gruesome reality but also for the layers of myth and legend that have enveloped it over the centuries. The narrative of the Beast is a complex tapestry of fear, superstition, and historical intrigue, reflecting the social and cultural milieu of 18th-century rural France.

The attacks attributed to the Beast began in the summer of 1764. The first known victim was a young woman named Jeanne Boulet, who was reportedly killed on June 30 near the village of Les Hubacs. Her death was followed by a spate of similar attacks in which the victims, predominantly women and children, were brutally mauled and often decapitated. The ferocity and frequency of these attacks were unprecedented, and the descriptions provided by survivors and witnesses painted a picture of a creature unlike any known predator. The Beast was typically described as a large, wolf-like animal with formidable jaws, a reddish fur streaked with black, a broad chest, and a long, sinuous tail. It was said to move with remarkable speed and agility, often attacking its victims with a savagery that left even seasoned hunters and soldiers in awe.

As the death toll mounted, fear and hysteria gripped the region. The remote and rugged terrain of Gévaudan, with its dense forests and isolated villages, created a perfect backdrop for the emergence of such a terrifying legend. The attacks often took place in secluded areas, making it difficult for the local authorities and villagers to mount an effective defense. Despite the concerted efforts of local hunters and the deployment of soldiers, the Beast seemed to elude capture, adding to its fearsome reputation. Its ability to evade traps and avoid armed confrontations led to speculation that it possessed supernatural qualities, further fueling the public's fear and fascination.

The response to the Beast's reign of terror was multifaceted, involving local hunters, military personnel, and even the intervention of the French monarchy. Initially, local efforts to hunt down the creature were hampered by the challenging terrain and the elusive nature of the Beast. Traditional hunting methods proved ineffective against an adversary that seemed to possess an almost preternatural intelligence and cunning. The failure to capture or kill the Beast only served to heighten the sense of dread and helplessness among the populace.

In response to the growing crisis, King Louis XV took a personal interest in the matter and dispatched professional wolf hunters and soldiers to Gévaudan. Among the most notable figures involved in the hunt was Jean-Charles-Marc-Antoine Vaumesle d'Enneval, a professional wolf hunter from Normandy, who arrived in early 1765 with his son and a team of trained dogs. Despite their considerable experience, the d'Ennevals were unable to bring down the Beast, and their efforts ended in frustration.

The hunt for the Beast reached its climax with the arrival of François Antoine, the king's lieutenant of the hunt, in the summer of 1765. Antoine, an experienced hunter and a member of the royal household, was tasked with eliminating the threat once and for all. On September 20, 1765, Antoine and his team managed to kill a large wolf-like animal in the forest of Chazes. The creature, which was unusually large and bore a striking resemblance to the descriptions of the Beast, was displayed with great ceremony and declared to be the infamous Beast of Gévaudan. The animal was sent to Versailles, where it was exhibited as proof of the successful hunt, and Antoine was hailed as a hero. However, despite the apparent resolution of the crisis, the attacks continued, suggesting that the true Beast had either evaded capture or that there were multiple creatures involved.

The saga of the Beast of Gévaudan did not end with the death of the creature killed by Antoine. The attacks persisted, and the mystery deepened as the number of victims continued to rise. The ongoing terror led to renewed efforts to hunt down the Beast, culminating in a significant event in June 1767. Jean Chastel, a local farmer and hunter, claimed to have killed the Beast on June 19, 1767, at Mont Mouchet. Chastel's account of the encounter was imbued with elements of folklore and religious symbolism, including the assertion that he had used a blessed silver bullet to bring down the creature. The body of the animal killed by Chastel was reportedly examined by several witnesses, including local officials and a surgeon, who confirmed that it matched the descriptions of the Beast. With Chastel's success, the attacks finally ceased, and the region of Gévaudan could begin to recover from the long ordeal.

The identity of the Beast of Gévaudan remains a subject of speculation and debate to this day. Various theories have been proposed, ranging from the plausible to the fantastical. Some historians and researchers believe that the Beast was a large wolf or a hybrid animal, possibly a cross between a wolf and a domestic dog. This theory is supported by the fact that wolves were common in the region during the 18th century, and attacks on humans, though rare, were not unheard of. The unusually aggressive behavior and the sheer number of victims, however, suggest that the Beast may have been an aberrant individual or an exotic animal introduced to the area, possibly as a result of human intervention.

Another theory posits that the Beast was a trained animal, perhaps an exotic species such as a hyena or a large predator kept by someone in the region. This theory is supported by the accounts of the Beast's unusual appearance and behavior, which differed from typical wolf attacks. Some researchers have suggested that the Beast may have been brought to Gévaudan by a traveler or an aristocrat with a private menagerie, adding an element of intrigue and human agency to the story.

The supernatural interpretation of the Beast as a creature with otherworldly origins has also persisted, reflecting the folkloric and mythological context of the time. The idea that the Beast was a demonic entity or a manifestation of divine retribution was a common theme in 18th-century folklore, and it resonated with the deeply religious and superstitious population of rural France. The involvement of figures like Jean Chastel, whose account of killing the Beast included elements of religious ritual and symbolism, further fueled these interpretations and cemented the Beast's place in the pantheon of legendary monsters.

The legacy of the Beast of Gévaudan extends beyond the realm of folklore and historical mystery. The story has inspired numerous works of literature, film, and art, becoming a cultural touchstone that continues to captivate the imagination. Among the most notable adaptations is the 2001 French film "Le Pacte des Loups" ("Brotherhood of the Wolf"), which combines elements of historical drama, horror, and fantasy to tell a fictionalized version of the Beast's story. The film's portrayal of the Beast as a supernatural creature, trained and controlled by a secret society, reflects the enduring fascination with the mystery and the blending of fact and fiction that characterizes the legend of the Beast.

The tale of the Beast of Gévaudan also provides a window into the social and cultural dynamics of 18th-century France. The fear and hysteria generated by the Beast's attacks highlight the anxieties and uncertainties of rural life in a period marked by political turmoil, economic hardship, and social change. The response to the Beast, including the involvement of the monarchy and the deployment of professional hunters, underscores the importance of authority and the central role of the state in addressing crises and maintaining order. The story also reflects the intersection of science, religion, and folklore in the understanding of natural phenomena and the interpretation of extraordinary events.

In contemporary times, the Beast of Gévaudan has become a symbol of the enduring power of myth and the fascination with the unknown. The story continues to attract the interest of researchers, historians, and paranormal enthusiasts, who seek to unravel the mystery and uncover the truth behind the legend. The region of Gévaudan, now a quiet and picturesque part of France, embraces its association with the Beast, with local museums, tours, and events celebrating the history and folklore of the infamous creature.

Chapter 35: The Edinburgh Vaults Hauntings

The Edinburgh Vaults, also known as the South Bridge Vaults, are a series of chambers formed in the nineteen arches of the South Bridge in Edinburgh, Scotland, which date back to the late 18th century. Initially constructed to house taverns, workshops, and storage spaces for merchants, these underground vaults quickly gained a more sinister reputation. Within a few decades, the businesses moved out, and the vaults became the city's underworld, sheltering the poorest inhabitants, illicit activities, and, as many believe, a significant amount of paranormal activity. The hauntings and strange occurrences reported in these vaults have intrigued both locals and paranormal enthusiasts for centuries.

The South Bridge itself was opened in 1788 and was an essential project to aid Edinburgh's expansion. The structure was designed with a series of chambers beneath it, which were intended to provide housing and workspaces for local businesses. However, due to the poor construction and lack of waterproofing, the vaults quickly began to suffer from dampness and became unsuitable for legitimate businesses. By the early 19th century, the merchants had abandoned the vaults, which then became a refuge for the city's poorest citizens, a place where illegal activities such as gambling, drinking, and prostitution thrived. The squalid conditions, coupled with high crime rates, made the vaults a place of misery and despair, which some believe have contributed to the haunting atmosphere that persists to this day.

The paranormal activity reported in the Edinburgh Vaults is varied and often chilling. Visitors and ghost hunters have reported hearing disembodied voices, whispers, and footsteps echoing through the dark corridors. Some have felt sudden drops in temperature, experienced the sensation of being watched, or even touched by unseen hands. One of the most frequently reported apparitions is that of a tall, imposing man often referred to as "Mr. Boots." This ghost is said to wear heavy boots that can be heard clomping through the corridors. His presence is often accompanied by a feeling of malevolence, and he is known to make his presence known by pushing or shoving visitors.

Another well-known spirit said to inhabit the vaults is that of a young boy named Jack. Unlike Mr. Boots, Jack is considered a more benevolent entity. Visitors have reported seeing him as a shadowy figure, feeling a small hand slipping into theirs, or hearing the sound of a child's laughter. Some believe Jack is the ghost of a child who lived and possibly died in the vaults during their use as a refuge for the city's poor.

The vaults also house the ghost of a cobbler who is believed to have died while working in his small workshop within the underground chambers. His spirit is often seen or sensed in the area where his shop once stood. The cobbler's ghost is usually described as non-threatening, simply going about his work, as if unaware of the passage of time and his own demise.

Many ghost hunting teams and paranormal investigators have conducted investigations within the Edinburgh Vaults, often with startling results. For instance, the show "Most Haunted" visited the site and reported experiencing a range of paranormal phenomena, including strange noises, unexplained movements, and physical sensations. Investigators from other groups have captured numerous EVPs (Electronic Voice Phenomena), which are believed to be the voices of spirits attempting to communicate with the living. These recordings often include voices speaking in English and sometimes in the Scots language, reflecting the historical usage of the vaults.

Psychics and mediums who have visited the vaults often describe an overwhelming sense of sadness and fear permeating the underground chambers. Many believe that the vaults have absorbed the negative energy from the suffering and violence that occurred there over the centuries. This residual energy is thought to be responsible for the hauntings, acting as a sort of spiritual echo of the past.

The Edinburgh Vaults have also been linked to more sinister and malevolent activities. During their time as a refuge for the city's criminal element, it is believed that numerous crimes, including murders, took place within the vaults. The bodies of victims may have been hidden in the dark recesses, never to be discovered. This association with death and violence has added to the vaults' haunted reputation, with some believing that the spirits of those who died violently remain trapped within the walls.

The vaults were rediscovered in the late 20th century after being closed off and forgotten for many years. Since their rediscovery, they have become a popular tourist attraction, with numerous ghost tours and paranormal investigations taking place regularly. Despite the commercialization, the eerie atmosphere of the vaults remains, and reports of strange occurrences continue to emerge.

The Edinburgh Vaults stand as a testament to the darker side of Edinburgh's history, a place where the past's suffering, crime, and death seem to have left an indelible mark on the fabric of the environment. Whether one believes in ghosts or not, the tales of paranormal activity and the haunted reputation of the vaults add a layer of mystery and intrigue to these historic chambers. The stories of Mr. Boots, little Jack, the cobbler, and the countless unidentified spirits contribute to the vaults' status as one of the most haunted locations in Scotland, attracting those who seek to experience the supernatural firsthand.

Chapter 36: The Case of Mary Reeser

The case of Mary Reeser is one of the most famous and baffling examples of alleged spontaneous human combustion (SHC) in modern history. Mary Hardy Reeser, a 67-year-old woman, was found deceased in her home in St. Petersburg, Florida, on July 2, 1951, in circumstances that have defied conventional explanation and sparked numerous theories about spontaneous human combustion.

On the evening of July 1, 1951, Mary Reeser was visited by her son, Dr. Richard Reeser, and her landlady, Pansy Carpenter. After their visit, Mary, who was known to be a smoker and was suffering from mild health issues, indicated that she was planning to take a couple of sleeping pills before going to bed. Dr. Reeser bid his mother goodnight and left, expecting nothing out of the ordinary. The following morning, Pansy Carpenter attempted to deliver a telegram to Mary but received no response. Noticing that the door handle was unusually warm, Carpenter became concerned and called the authorities.

When the firemen and police arrived, they found a scene that was both disturbing and perplexing. Mary Reeser's body had been almost entirely incinerated, leaving only a portion of her left foot still in its slipper, part of her backbone, and her shrunken skull. The chair in which she had been sitting was also heavily damaged by the fire. However, the rest of the room, and indeed the entire apartment, showed minimal signs of fire damage. Some plastic items in the room had softened and melted, and there was a light soot covering, but there was no extensive burning or charring as one might expect from a fire intense enough to cremate a human body.

The local police were baffled and quickly escalated the investigation to higher authorities, including the FBI. The case attracted national attention and brought experts from various fields to try to determine what had happened. Despite extensive investigation, including the involvement of Dr. Wilton M. Krogman, a professor of physical anthropology and a recognized expert on fire and its effects on the human body, no definitive conclusion could be reached. Dr. Krogman, in particular, was struck by the anomalies of the case. He noted that in his extensive experience with fire victims, he had never seen a body so completely consumed by flames without causing significant damage to the surrounding environment. The intense heat required to reduce a body to ash, as seen in crematoriums, would typically require temperatures around 2500 degrees Fahrenheit sustained for several hours, conditions that would undoubtedly have led to far more extensive damage to the apartment.

One of the prevailing theories at the time was that Mary Reeser might have accidentally set herself on fire with a cigarette while in a sedated state from the sleeping pills she had taken. This hypothesis suggests that the combination of her body fat, the flammable nature of her clothing, and the confined space of the chair could have created a "wick effect," wherein her body fat served as a fuel source, burning at a high temperature over several hours. This theory, however, still struggled to explain the lack of significant damage to the surrounding environment and the highly localized nature of the fire.

The concept of spontaneous human combustion, where a human body ignites without an apparent external source of ignition, has been a topic of fascination and debate for centuries. Proponents of the SHC theory argue that there might be unknown biochemical processes within the human body that could lead to such an event. Some hypotheses have suggested the possibility of acetone buildup in the body, which is highly flammable, or other chemical reactions that could generate enough heat to ignite the body. However, there is no scientific consensus on the validity of these theories, and spontaneous human combustion remains largely in the realm of the unexplained.

The case of Mary Reeser also brought to light other historical accounts of similar mysterious deaths, where victims were found incinerated in a manner that defied conventional explanation. These cases often share common features: the victims are typically older adults, often with some mobility issues, and the fires are highly localized, with the surrounding environment showing little evidence of the intense heat required to reduce a human body to ash.

Despite the passage of time and advancements in forensic science, the case of Mary Reeser remains unsolved. It continues to be cited in discussions and studies about spontaneous human combustion, serving as a cautionary tale of the limits of our understanding of certain phenomena. The meticulous documentation of the case, including photographs, reports, and testimonies, ensures that it remains a significant point of reference for researchers and enthusiasts of the unexplained.

Mary Reeser's tragic death is a poignant reminder of how some mysteries endure, resisting easy explanations. It invites us to consider the potential limits of our current scientific knowledge and the possibility that there may be natural phenomena we have yet to fully understand. Whether her death was a rare but natural occurrence, an example of spontaneous human combustion, or the result of some other as-yet-unknown factor, it stands as one of the most enigmatic and unsettling events in the annals of forensic history. The legacy of Mary Reeser's case lives on, fueling both scientific inquiry and the human fascination with the unknown, prompting a deeper exploration of the mysteries that lie at the intersection of biology, chemistry, and perhaps the supernatural.

Chapter 37: The Haunted Chateau de Brissac

The Château de Brissac, located in the picturesque Loire Valley of France, is renowned not only for its grandiose architecture and historical significance but also for its reputation as one of the most haunted castles in Europe. The château's haunting is deeply intertwined with its tumultuous history, marked by tales of love, betrayal, and violence that have left an indelible mark on the property and contributed to its ghostly lore.

Originally constructed in the 11th century by the Counts of Anjou, the Château de Brissac underwent significant expansions and renovations over the centuries, particularly during the Renaissance period. The castle as it stands today is a remarkable example of French Renaissance architecture, boasting seven floors, 204 rooms, and a host of grand halls and lavishly decorated interiors. However, beneath its opulent exterior lies a darker history that has given rise to numerous ghost stories and eerie legends.

The most famous and enduring ghost story associated with Château de Brissac centers around the tragic figure of Charlotte de Brézé, who is often referred to as the "Green Lady." Charlotte was the illegitimate daughter of King Charles VII and his mistress, Agnès Sorel. She was married to Jacques de Brézé, a nobleman who owned the château in the late 15th century. Their marriage was far from happy, marred by Charlotte's infidelity and Jacques's jealousy.

According to legend, Charlotte engaged in a clandestine affair with a local huntsman. One fateful night, Jacques discovered the lovers together in Charlotte's bedchamber. Enraged by the betrayal, Jacques is said to have murdered both Charlotte and her lover in a fit of violent passion. The gruesome event left a lasting imprint on the château, and it is believed that Charlotte's restless spirit has haunted the property ever since.

Visitors and residents of Château de Brissac have reported numerous encounters with the Green Lady over the centuries. She is often described as wearing a green dress, hence her moniker, and her apparition is frequently seen wandering the halls and staircases of the castle. Her face is said to be disfigured, reflecting the violent manner of her death, and her presence is often accompanied by a chilling sense of unease. Some have reported hearing her moans and whispers in the dead of night, adding to the castle's eerie atmosphere.

In addition to the Green Lady, the château is reputed to be haunted by several other spectral inhabitants. These include soldiers who perished in battles during the castle's long history and former servants who remain tied to their earthly duties. The château's extensive wine cellars, in particular, are said to be a hotspot for paranormal activity, with reports of shadowy figures and inexplicable cold spots.

The château's haunted reputation was further cemented by the accounts of its owners and guests. In the early 20th century, the Marquis de Brissac, a descendant of Jacques de Brézé, documented several strange occurrences in the castle. He recounted hearing footsteps in empty corridors, doors slamming shut on their own, and objects moving inexplicably. His accounts were corroborated by visitors, who also reported witnessing apparitions and experiencing unexplained phenomena.

The legend of the Green Lady and the château's haunted status have made Château de Brissac a popular destination for tourists and paranormal enthusiasts alike. Many come hoping to catch a glimpse of the ethereal figure or to experience the castle's ghostly ambiance firsthand. The current owners, the de Cossé-Brissac family, who have resided in the château for generations, have embraced its haunted heritage, offering ghost tours and hosting events that celebrate its spooky reputation.

Beyond its ghost stories, Château de Brissac is steeped in rich history and cultural significance. It played a crucial role during the Wars of Religion in France, serving as a stronghold for the Catholic League. The château was besieged and damaged during the conflict, leading to extensive repairs and renovations in the subsequent years. Its historical importance and architectural splendor have earned it a place among the most notable châteaux in the Loire Valley.

The haunted Château de Brissac also serves as a testament to the enduring power of folklore and the human fascination with the supernatural. The tales of the Green Lady and other ghostly inhabitants continue to captivate the imagination, drawing people from all over the world to explore its haunted halls. Whether one believes in ghosts or not, there is no denying that the château's atmosphere, steeped in history and legend, creates a compelling and unforgettable experience.

Over the years, the château has been the subject of numerous investigations by paranormal researchers and ghost hunters. Teams equipped with modern ghost-hunting equipment have sought to capture evidence of the supernatural within its ancient walls. While some have reported capturing strange anomalies, such as unexplained shadows and EVPs (Electronic Voice Phenomena), definitive proof of the hauntings remains elusive, adding to the mystique and allure of Château de Brissac.

Chapter 38: The Devil's Footprints

The Devil's Footprints, also known as the "Devil's Hoofmarks," refer to a mysterious and unexplained phenomenon that occurred in Devon, England, in February 1855. This event has puzzled historians, researchers, and paranormal enthusiasts for over a century and a half, and it remains one of the most intriguing and enigmatic episodes in the annals of unexplained phenomena.

The incident began on the night of February 8-9, 1855, when heavy snowfall blanketed the region. The following morning, the residents of Devon awoke to find a series of strange, hoof-like tracks in the snow. These footprints, measuring approximately 4 inches long and 3 inches wide, appeared to have been made by a bipedal creature. The tracks were unusual not only in their shape but also in their distribution. They were found in a single-file line, as if made by a creature walking on two legs rather than four, and they extended over a vast distance of around 40 to 100 miles, cutting through various types of terrain.

The footprints were reported in numerous towns and villages across Devon, including Exmouth, Topsham, Dawlish, and Teignmouth. They traversed rooftops, crossed rivers, and climbed over high walls and haystacks, as if the creature making them could walk through or over obstacles with ease. This incredible mobility led many to speculate that the tracks were not of this world, and the idea that they were the work of the Devil himself quickly gained traction among the superstitious population.

Local newspapers, including the *Exeter and Plymouth Gazette*, documented the strange phenomenon, and the story soon spread beyond Devon, capturing the imagination of the entire country. The prints were described as resembling a cloven hoof, similar to those of a donkey or mule, but the manner in which they were laid out—perfectly aligned and in a straight line—defied logical explanation. The widespread coverage and the sheer mystery of the event led to a flurry of theories and speculations.

One of the earliest theories proposed that the tracks were made by a variety of animals, including badgers, otters, or even kangaroos. However, these explanations were quickly dismissed due to the consistent shape and size of the footprints and the remarkable distances they covered. Additionally, the footprints were found in places that these animals could not easily access, such as rooftops and enclosed courtyards.

Another popular theory suggested that the footprints were a hoax perpetrated by pranksters. Some believed that individuals with stilts or specially made shoes could have created the tracks. However, the sheer scale of the phenomenon, covering such a vast area in a single night, made this explanation highly improbable. Moreover, no evidence of such a hoax was ever discovered.

Some researchers speculated that the tracks were caused by natural phenomena. One theory proposed that the unusual footprints were the result of a rare weather condition known as "ball lightning." According to this theory, the ball lightning might have created a series of scorch marks in the snow, giving the appearance of hoof-like prints. However, there was no concrete evidence to support this hypothesis, and it did not account for the precise and uniform shape of the footprints.

In the absence of a satisfactory scientific explanation, supernatural and paranormal theories flourished. Many locals believed that the Devil himself had visited Devon, leaving his footprints as a sign of his presence. This belief was reinforced by the footprints' resemblance to cloven hooves, traditionally associated with the Devil in folklore and religious iconography. The idea of the Devil wandering the countryside in the dead of night struck fear into the hearts of many, adding a chilling layer to the mystery.

Over the years, the Devil's Footprints have continued to intrigue and mystify. In the early 20th century, paranormal investigator Elliott

O'Donnell examined the case and concluded that the tracks were likely made by an unknown supernatural entity. O'Donnell's investigations, along with those of other paranormal researchers, have kept the legend of the Devil's Footprints alive in popular culture.

Modern researchers have revisited the phenomenon, offering new hypotheses based on advances in science and technology. Some have suggested that the tracks could have been caused by an unusual atmospheric condition or a rare animal behavior that has yet to be documented. Others have proposed that the footprints were the result of a mass hallucination or collective delusion, fueled by the superstitions and fears of the time.

Despite these efforts, the true origin of the Devil's Footprints remains a mystery. The lack of definitive evidence and the sheer improbability of many of the proposed explanations have left the phenomenon in the realm of the unexplained. The incident has become a classic case study in the field of cryptozoology and paranormal investigation, illustrating the enduring power of mysterious and unexplained events to captivate the human imagination.

The Devil's Footprints also serve as a reminder of the limitations of human understanding and the complexity of the natural world. Even in an age of advanced science and technology, there are still phenomena that defy explanation, challenging our assumptions and inviting us to explore the boundaries of knowledge. The footprints' enduring mystery underscores the fact that there are still many aspects of our world that remain unexplained, waiting to be discovered and understood.

In popular culture, the Devil's Footprints have inspired numerous books, articles, and documentaries, each exploring different facets of the mystery and offering new interpretations. The incident has become a staple of folklore and a symbol of the unexplained, resonating with those who are fascinated by the unknown and the supernatural.

Chapter 39: The Ghosts of Eastern State Penitentiary

Eastern State Penitentiary, located in Philadelphia, Pennsylvania, is one of the most famous and historically significant prisons in the United States. It opened in 1829 and was operational until 1971. Its unique architecture and innovative approach to incarceration made it a model for over 300 prisons worldwide. However, it is perhaps best known today for its reputation as one of the most haunted places in America. The ghosts of Eastern State Penitentiary are said to haunt its crumbling cellblocks and corridors, attracting paranormal investigators and curious visitors from around the world.

Eastern State Penitentiary was designed by architect John Haviland and opened its doors on October 25, 1829. It was one of the first prisons to implement the concept of solitary confinement, an experiment intended to encourage penitence and reform among inmates. Each prisoner was kept in a separate cell, isolated from others, with only a small exercise yard for brief, solitary outdoor time. The design featured seven main cellblocks radiating from a central hub, resembling a wagon wheel, which allowed guards to monitor the entire facility from a single point. This layout, known as the "Pennsylvania System," was groundbreaking at the time.

While the intention behind the prison's design was to foster reflection and rehabilitation, the reality was far more brutal. Solitary confinement led to severe psychological effects on inmates, many of whom suffered from depression, anxiety, and hallucinations. The harsh conditions and extreme isolation have been cited as factors contributing to the penitentiary's haunted reputation. The echoes of suffering and despair from those incarcerated within its walls seem to linger, manifesting as ghostly apparitions and unexplained phenomena.

One of the most famous ghost stories associated with Eastern State Penitentiary involves Al Capone, the notorious gangster. Capone was incarcerated at Eastern State from 1929 to 1930, serving time for carrying a concealed, deadly weapon. During his stay, Capone occupied a relatively luxurious cell compared to the others, furnished with a desk, a lamp, paintings, and a radio. Despite these comforts, Capone reportedly experienced tormenting visions and ghostly encounters. He claimed to be haunted by the ghost of James Clark, one of the victims of the St. Valentine's Day Massacre, orchestrated by Capone's gang. Capone's cell is now one of the most visited spots in the penitentiary, with many visitors and staff reporting strange occurrences and feelings of unease.

Cellblock 12 is another area notorious for paranormal activity. It is said to be one of the most haunted parts of the penitentiary, with numerous reports of disembodied laughter, shadowy figures, and eerie whispers. Visitors and paranormal investigators have described hearing the sounds of cell doors slamming shut and anguished cries echoing through the empty corridors. Some have even claimed to see apparitions of former inmates, their spectral forms wandering the cellblock as if still trapped in their cells.

Cellblock 4 is also known for its ghostly inhabitants. Reports from this area include the sighting of a shadowy figure that darts around corners and down hallways. This apparition has been seen by both visitors and staff, often disappearing through walls or into empty cells. In addition to visual sightings, there are frequent reports of unexplained noises, such as footsteps and indistinct murmuring, contributing to the area's reputation for being haunted.

Cellblock 6 is home to yet another famous ghostly figure. A shadowy silhouette, often described as a dark, human-like shape, has been seen standing at the end of the hallway or peering out from the cells. This figure is said to move silently and disappear when approached. Witnesses have reported feeling an intense, oppressive presence when near this shadowy figure, leading many to believe it is a residual haunting—a lingering imprint of the past trauma experienced by the prisoners.

The prison's death row, known as "The Hole," is another hotspot for paranormal activity. This area was used for solitary confinement, where inmates endured the harshest conditions, often spending weeks in complete darkness. The oppressive atmosphere and the intense suffering experienced by those confined here are believed to have left a powerful residual energy. Visitors to The Hole often report feeling extreme cold spots, a sense of being watched, and a heavy, suffocating atmosphere. Some have also heard unexplained noises, such as knocks, bangs, and even distant screams.

One of the most compelling pieces of evidence of the penitentiary's haunted nature comes from paranormal investigators who have conducted extensive research within its walls. Many teams have captured EVPs (Electronic Voice Phenomena), recordings that seem to contain voices and sounds not heard during the investigation. These EVPs have included cries for help, indistinct conversations, and even names being spoken. Some investigators have also recorded visual anomalies, such as orbs of light, strange mists, and unexplained shadows.

The experiences of staff members and tour guides add further credence to the tales of hauntings. Many have reported encountering ghostly figures during their daily routines. For instance, some have seen the apparition of a guard in old-fashioned uniform patrolling the corridors. Others have encountered the spirits of former inmates, appearing briefly before vanishing. These sightings often occur in broad daylight, suggesting that the ghosts of Eastern State Penitentiary are not bound by the usual conventions of the supernatural.

The penitentiary has also been the subject of numerous television shows and documentaries exploring its haunted reputation. Programs such as "Ghost Hunters," "Ghost Adventures," and "Most Haunted" have featured Eastern State Penitentiary, documenting their investigations and capturing compelling evidence of paranormal activity. These shows have brought the haunted history of Eastern State to a global audience, further cementing its status as one of the most haunted locations in the world.

In addition to its haunted reputation, Eastern State Penitentiary is a significant historical landmark. It has been preserved as a National Historic Landmark and is open to the public for tours. The penitentiary offers both historical tours, which focus on its architectural and social significance, and ghost tours, which delve into its paranormal activity. The annual "Terror Behind the Walls" event, held around Halloween, transforms the penitentiary into a massive haunted house attraction, drawing thousands of visitors eager to experience the eerie ambiance and possibly encounter a ghost or two.

Eastern State Penitentiary stands as a testament to the complex and often dark history of the American penal system. Its innovative design and approach to incarceration were both groundbreaking and deeply flawed, leading to immense suffering for many of its inmates. The hauntings that are said to persist within its walls serve as a chilling reminder of this troubled past. Whether one believes in ghosts or not, there is no denying that Eastern State Penitentiary exudes an atmosphere of mystery and unease, making it a fascinating destination for those interested in history, architecture, and the paranormal.

Chapter 40: The Legend of the Flying Dutchman

The legend of the Flying Dutchman is one of the most enduring maritime ghost stories, deeply rooted in the folklore of the sea. It is the tale of a ghost ship that is doomed to sail the oceans for eternity, never able to make port, and is often seen as a bad omen by sailors. The story has evolved over centuries, with various versions and embellishments adding to its mystique. At its core, the legend speaks to the fears and superstitions of sailors facing the perils of the open sea.

The origins of the Flying Dutchman legend can be traced back to the 17th century during the Age of Sail, a period when European exploration and maritime trade were at their peak. The tale is said to have originated among Dutch sailors and quickly spread throughout the maritime world. The earliest recorded references to the Flying Dutchman date back to the late 18th century, although it is likely that the story was told orally for many years before being documented.

According to the most popular version of the legend, the Flying Dutchman was a Dutch ship captained by a man named Hendrick van der Decken. The name "Flying Dutchman" is believed to be a reference to the nationality of the ship and its crew. Captain van der Decken was a skilled and determined seaman who was known for his stubbornness and defiance of natural and supernatural forces alike.

The story goes that during a voyage around the Cape of Good Hope, a notoriously treacherous stretch of water off the southern tip of Africa, Captain van der Decken encountered a severe storm. Despite the pleas of his crew to turn back, the captain swore that he would sail around the Cape, even if it took him until Judgment Day. Some versions of the legend suggest that van der Decken made a pact with the Devil, promising his soul in exchange for safe passage.

As the storm raged on, the crew mutinied, desperate to escape the doomed voyage. In a fit of rage, van der Decken killed the leader of the mutiny and threw his body overboard. At that moment, a ghostly apparition appeared, condemning the captain and his ship to sail the seas forever, never to reach port or find rest. The crew was cursed along with the captain, doomed to share his fate for eternity.

The Flying Dutchman became a spectral ship, often described as a glowing or ghostly vessel seen sailing with full sails even in the most violent storms. Sailors who encountered the ship reported that it seemed to glide above the water rather than sail upon it, and that it emitted an eerie, otherworldly glow. The sighting of the Flying Dutchman was considered an ill omen, foretelling disaster or death for those who saw it.

Over the years, numerous sightings of the Flying Dutchman have been reported by sailors and explorers. One of the most famous accounts comes from Prince George of Wales, later King George V of the United Kingdom, who, as a young man, claimed to have seen the ghost ship while serving in the Royal Navy in 1881. According to his diary, the prince and several other crew members observed a ghostly vessel glowing with a red light, which vanished as they approached.

The legend of the Flying Dutchman has inspired countless literary and artistic works. In literature, one of the earliest references to the ghost ship appears in the 1795 book "Voyage to Botany Bay" by George Barrington. The tale was further popularized by the 1833 poem "The Flying Dutchman" by Thomas Moore and the 1843 opera "Der fliegende Holländer" by Richard Wagner. Wagner's opera, in particular, solidified the image of the cursed captain and his ghostly ship in the popular imagination.

The Flying Dutchman has also appeared in numerous novels, short stories, and films. One notable example is Washington Irving's 1824 short story "The Flying Dutchman on Tappan Sea," which adapts the legend to the Hudson River in New York. The ship has been featured in various works of fiction, from adventure novels to horror stories, each adding new elements and interpretations to the legend.

In popular culture, the Flying Dutchman has been depicted in films such as Disney's "Pirates of the Caribbean" series. In these movies, the ship is captained by the fearsome Davy Jones, who, along with his cursed crew, is bound to serve the ship for eternity. The portrayal of the Flying Dutchman in these films combines elements of the original legend with imaginative new details, such as the ship's ability to sail both above and below the water.

The enduring appeal of the Flying Dutchman legend can be attributed to several factors. First and foremost is the universal human fear of being lost and unable to find one's way home. The idea of a ship and its crew condemned to sail the oceans forever taps into deep-seated anxieties about isolation, helplessness, and the unknown. For sailors, who often faced dangerous and unpredictable conditions, the legend of the Flying Dutchman served as a powerful cautionary tale about the perils of defying nature and fate.

The ghost ship also embodies the idea of eternal punishment, a theme that resonates across various cultures and religious traditions. The curse placed upon Captain van der Decken and his crew can be seen as a form of divine retribution for their hubris and defiance. This aspect of the legend aligns with moralistic tales that warn against pride, disobedience, and making pacts with dark forces.

Moreover, the mysterious and supernatural elements of the Flying Dutchman story have captivated the imaginations of storytellers and audiences alike. The image of a ghostly ship sailing through stormy seas, glowing with an unearthly light, creates a vivid and haunting visual that lends itself well to dramatic retellings and artistic interpretations.

In maritime folklore, the Flying Dutchman has come to symbolize the ultimate in nautical mysteries. Despite advances in navigation and technology, the vastness and unpredictability of the sea continue to inspire awe and fear. The legend of the Flying Dutchman serves as a reminder of the sea's power and the limitations of human control over the natural world.

Modern interpretations of the Flying Dutchman legend often blend historical accounts with imaginative speculation. Some researchers have attempted to find real-life counterparts to the story, exploring historical records for ships that may have inspired the legend. Others have delved into the psychological and cultural factors that have sustained the tale over centuries, examining how it reflects the fears and values of different societies.

In addition to its literary and cultural significance, the Flying Dutchman legend has also had an impact on nautical lore and traditions. Sailors continue to share ghost stories and superstitions, and the sighting of a ghost ship like the Flying Dutchman remains a potent symbol of bad luck and impending doom. The legend is also referenced in various maritime rituals and customs, such as the practice of avoiding certain areas or taking precautions during dangerous weather conditions.

Chapter 41: The Whaley House Hauntings

The Whaley House, located in San Diego, California, is often heralded as one of the most haunted houses in the United States. Built in 1857 by Thomas Whaley, this historic home has a storied past filled with tragedy, scandal, and supernatural occurrences. The house has garnered significant attention from paranormal investigators, historians, and curious visitors drawn to its reputation for ghostly activity. The Whaley House is not just a museum of San Diego's early history but also a reputed hotspot for paranormal phenomena.

Thomas Whaley, a New York native, moved to California during the Gold Rush in the mid-19th century, seeking fortune and new opportunities. In 1857, he built the Whaley House in the Old Town area of San Diego, using bricks from his own brickyard. The house served multiple purposes over the years: it was not only the Whaley family residence but also housed San Diego's first commercial theater, a granary, a general store, and the county courthouse. Given its diverse uses, the house became a central hub of activity in Old Town San Diego.

Before the Whaley House was constructed, the land on which it stands had already been the site of several traumatic events. Most notably, it was the location of the public execution of James "Yankee Jim" Robinson in 1852. Robinson was convicted of grand larceny and sentenced to death by hanging. His execution was particularly brutal, with accounts suggesting that Robinson did not die quickly, but rather struggled and choked to death. Thomas Whaley, present at the hanging, later purchased the land, perhaps unaware or dismissive of the potential for the lingering spirits of its past occupants.

The Whaley family itself was plagued by tragedy. Shortly after moving into the house, Thomas and his wife, Anna, experienced the death of their 18-month-old son, Thomas Whaley Jr., due to scarlet fever. This loss was devastating to the family and marked the beginning of a series of unfortunate events. Over the years, several more family members died in the house, including Anna Whaley herself and her daughter, Violet Whaley, who committed suicide in 1885 after a failed marriage.

Violet's story is particularly tragic. She had married a man who turned out to be a con artist. Abandoned and disgraced, Violet returned to the Whaley House in deep depression. Her mental anguish led her to take her own life by shooting herself in the chest. Her suicide note, a sorrowful reflection on her despair, underscores the profound sadness that permeated the Whaley family. This series of personal tragedies is said to contribute significantly to the house's haunted reputation.

The Whaley House's haunted history began to attract attention in the early 20th century. Reports of ghostly apparitions, strange noises, and unexplained phenomena started to emerge, drawing the interest of paranormal investigators and curious visitors alike. Over the years, numerous sightings and encounters have been documented, adding to the lore and mystique of the house.

One of the most commonly reported apparitions is that of Thomas Whaley himself. Visitors and staff have described seeing a tall man in period clothing, believed to be Thomas, wandering the halls and rooms of the house. His presence is often accompanied by the smell of tobacco smoke, which is said to be a signature of his ghostly visits. People have also reported feeling a sudden drop in temperature when his spirit is near.

Anna Whaley, Thomas's wife, is another frequent ghostly presence. Her apparition is often seen in the garden or sitting in her favorite rocking chair. Visitors have reported feeling a comforting presence and the scent of lavender, which was known to be Anna's favorite perfume.

Some have even claimed to hear the faint sound of a piano playing, as Anna was an accomplished pianist in her lifetime.

The spirit of Yankee Jim Robinson, the man hanged on the property before the Whaley House was built, is another well-documented haunting. Robinson's ghost is often described as a tall, shadowy figure that lurks in the house's darker corners. Visitors have reported hearing heavy footsteps, believed to be Robinson's, echoing through the halls. Some have felt an oppressive, malevolent energy associated with his spirit, which contrasts with the more benign presences of the Whaley family members.

Violet Whaley's tragic suicide has also left an indelible mark on the house's paranormal activity. Her spirit is often felt in the second-floor bedrooms, where she spent much of her time in despair. Visitors have reported hearing soft weeping and feeling an overwhelming sense of sadness when entering these rooms. Some have even seen the ghostly figure of a young woman in a long dress, believed to be Violet, standing by the window or sitting on the bed.

In addition to these well-known apparitions, the Whaley House is also home to numerous other ghostly phenomena. Disembodied voices, laughter, and music are frequently heard throughout the house. Objects have been known to move on their own, doors open and close without explanation, and cold spots are commonly felt in various rooms. The staircase, in particular, is a hotspot for paranormal activity, with many visitors reporting a sense of being watched or followed as they ascend or descend the steps.

Paranormal investigators have conducted numerous investigations at the Whaley House, using a variety of tools and techniques to document the activity. EVP (Electronic Voice Phenomena) recordings have captured ghostly voices, including what some believe to be the voices of the Whaley family members. Photographs and videos have revealed unexplained shadows and orbs of light, and motion sensors have detected movement in empty rooms. These findings have only served to bolster the house's reputation as a center of paranormal activity.

The Whaley House has also been featured on numerous television shows and documentaries about haunted places. Programs like "Ghost Adventures," "Most Haunted," and "America's Most Haunted Places" have all explored the Whaley House, bringing its ghostly legends to a wider audience. These shows often include dramatic reenactments of the house's haunted history, interviews with witnesses, and live investigations that aim to capture evidence of the supernatural.

In addition to its haunted reputation, the Whaley House is a significant historical landmark. It was designated a California Historical Landmark in 1932 and is now maintained by the Save Our Heritage Organisation (SOHO). The house has been preserved to reflect its 19th-century origins, with period furnishings and decor that give visitors a glimpse into San Diego's early history. Guided tours of the house provide a detailed account of the Whaley family's life, the house's multifaceted uses, and its haunted legacy.

The Whaley House continues to attract thousands of visitors each year, drawn by its rich history and ghostly reputation. It serves as a powerful reminder of the enduring impact of personal tragedy and the mysteries of the supernatural. Whether one believes in ghosts or not, the Whaley House offers a fascinating glimpse into the past and the lingering echoes of those who once lived there.

Chapter 42: The Curse of the Hope Diamond

The Hope Diamond is one of the most famous and storied gemstones in the world, renowned not only for its extraordinary size, deep blue color, and unparalleled beauty but also for the curse that is said to accompany it. The legend of the Hope Diamond's curse has captivated people for generations, weaving a tale of misfortune, mystery, and intrigue around this precious stone. Its history is a rich tapestry of fact and fiction, involving royalty, theft, and untimely deaths. To fully appreciate the depth of the Hope Diamond's curse, one must delve into its origins, its journey through history, and the lives it has touched along the way.

The story of the Hope Diamond begins in the 17th century, in the mines of Golconda in India, renowned for producing some of the world's finest diamonds. The diamond that would eventually become the Hope Diamond was originally a much larger stone, weighing an estimated 112 carats. This rough diamond was purchased by the French gem merchant Jean-Baptiste Tavernier, who brought it back to Europe. Tavernier sold the diamond to King Louis XIV of France in 1668, who had it cut into a 67.1-carat gem known as the "French Blue" or "Blue Diamond of the Crown."

The French Blue was set into a royal pendant and became part of the French crown jewels. It was worn by Louis XIV and subsequent French monarchs, including Louis XV and Louis XVI. The diamond's association with the French royal family is one of the earliest links in the chain of events that would give rise to its cursed reputation. During the French Revolution, the crown jewels, including the French Blue, were stolen in a dramatic heist in 1792. The diamond disappeared for several decades, during which time it was likely recut to prevent recognition and to increase its value.

The diamond resurfaced in the early 19th century, now weighing approximately 45.52 carats and with a deep blue color. It was acquired by the London banking family of Hope in 1839, from whom it derives its current name. Henry Philip Hope, a gem collector and member of the prominent Hope banking family, purchased the diamond, and it became a centerpiece of his collection. The diamond's presence in the Hope family coincided with a period of financial decline, leading to rumors that the gem brought misfortune to its owners.

The legend of the Hope Diamond's curse gained further traction in the early 20th century. Stories began to circulate that the diamond had been stolen from a sacred Hindu temple idol, leading to a curse on anyone who possessed it. While there is no historical evidence to support this claim, the tale added an air of mystique and danger to the already famous gem. Journalists, jewelers, and storytellers embellished the story, linking the diamond to a series of tragic events and untimely deaths.

One of the most notorious aspects of the Hope Diamond's curse is the list of supposed victims who suffered misfortune after coming into contact with the gem. While many of these stories are anecdotal and lack concrete evidence, they have nonetheless contributed to the diamond's fearsome reputation. Among the most frequently cited victims is Princess de Lamballe, a close friend of Marie Antoinette. The princess was brutally murdered during the French Revolution, and some accounts suggest she may have been a victim of the curse, despite the lack of direct evidence linking her to the diamond.

Another often-mentioned victim is Jacques Colot, a French merchant who is said to have owned the diamond briefly in the early 19th century. According to legend, Colot went mad and committed suicide after acquiring the gem. However, historical records do not corroborate this story, and it is likely an embellishment added to the diamond's mythos.

Evelyn Walsh McLean, an American socialite, is one of the more well-documented owners of the Hope Diamond. She purchased the gem from the famous jeweler Pierre Cartier in 1911. McLean, who had a penchant for extravagant jewelry, wore the diamond frequently and even had it mounted in a striking platinum setting surrounded by white diamonds. Despite her initial delight with the gem, McLean's life was marked by a series of personal tragedies. Her firstborn son was killed in a car accident at the age of nine, her daughter died of a drug overdose at 25, and her husband, Edward Beale McLean, suffered from mental illness and was eventually institutionalized. Evelyn herself passed away in 1947, and her estate was forced to sell the diamond to cover debts. These events have often been cited as evidence of the diamond's curse.

After Evelyn Walsh McLean's death, the Hope Diamond was purchased by the jeweler Harry Winston. Winston did not believe in the curse and often used the diamond in charity events and exhibitions. In 1958, he donated the Hope Diamond to the Smithsonian Institution, where it remains on display today. Since its arrival at the Smithsonian, the diamond has been viewed by millions of visitors and has become one of the museum's most popular exhibits.

The Hope Diamond's time at the Smithsonian has been largely free of the dramatic misfortunes that marked its earlier history. However, stories of the curse persist, often revived by media reports and fictional portrayals. The diamond's association with tragedy and mystery continues to captivate the public imagination, ensuring that its legend endures.

In addition to its storied past, the Hope Diamond is also a remarkable gem from a scientific perspective. Its deep blue color is due to trace amounts of boron within its crystal structure, and it exhibits a unique red phosphorescence when exposed to ultraviolet light. These characteristics have made the diamond a subject of study for gemologists and scientists, adding another layer of fascination to its already complex history.

The Hope Diamond has also been the subject of numerous books, documentaries, and fictional works. It has appeared in various cultural contexts, from novels and films to television shows and even comic books. These portrayals often emphasize the diamond's beauty and supposed curse, blending fact and fiction to create compelling narratives that continue to intrigue audiences.

Chapter 43: The Ghosts of Waverly Hills Sanatorium

Waverly Hills Sanatorium, located in Louisville, Kentucky, is widely regarded as one of the most haunted locations in the United States. This imposing structure, originally built to treat patients suffering from tuberculosis, has become synonymous with ghost stories, paranormal investigations, and eerie legends. Its history is marked by tragedy and suffering, which many believe have left an indelible imprint of spectral activity on the premises. The ghosts of Waverly Hills Sanatorium are said to include former patients, nurses, and other staff members, their spirits lingering in the corridors and rooms where they once lived, worked, and died.

The history of Waverly Hills Sanatorium begins in the early 20th century, during a time when tuberculosis, also known as the "White Plague," was rampant and incurable. In 1910, a small two-story hospital was constructed on the site to treat tuberculosis patients. However, as the disease spread and the number of patients increased, it became clear that a larger facility was needed. Construction of the current Waverly Hills Sanatorium began in 1924, and the building was officially opened in 1926. This new facility was a state-of-the-art hospital designed to accommodate over 400 patients and was equipped with the latest medical technology of the time.

The sanatorium operated as a tuberculosis hospital until 1961, during which time thousands of patients passed through its doors. Tuberculosis was a highly contagious and often fatal disease, and the treatments available at the time were rudimentary at best. Patients at Waverly Hills were subjected to a variety of treatments, many of which were experimental and invasive. These included thoracoplasty, a painful surgical procedure to remove ribs and allow the lungs to expand, and pneumothorax, the intentional collapsing of a lung to "rest" it. While some treatments were aimed at curing the disease, others were simply palliative, intended to make patients more comfortable in their final days.

The mortality rate at Waverly Hills was high, and it is estimated that tens of thousands of patients died there over the years. The high death toll and the suffering experienced by patients have contributed to the building's reputation as a place of intense paranormal activity. One of the most infamous features of Waverly Hills is the "body chute," a long tunnel that was used to transport deceased patients from the hospital to the bottom of the hill, where they could be discreetly removed. This tunnel was intended to keep the sight of dead bodies from disturbing the other patients and to maintain morale, but it has since become a focal point for ghost stories and paranormal investigations.

The ghosts of Waverly Hills Sanatorium are numerous and varied, with reports of apparitions, shadow figures, disembodied voices, and unexplained sounds being commonplace. One of the most frequently reported ghosts is that of a little boy named Timmy. Visitors and paranormal investigators have reported seeing the apparition of a young boy playing with a ball in the hallways and rooms of the sanatorium. The sound of a ball bouncing is often heard, and some have even seen the ball move on its own. Timmy is believed to be the spirit of a young patient who died at the hospital, and his playful presence is a poignant reminder of the many children who suffered and died at Waverly Hills.

Another well-known ghost is that of a nurse who is said to have committed suicide in Room 502. According to legend, in the 1920s, a nurse was found dead in this room, having hanged herself from a light fixture. It is believed that she was pregnant and unmarried, and the stigma and shame associated with her situation led her to take her own life. Visitors to Room 502 have reported feeling a sense of sadness and despair, and some have seen the apparition of a nurse in old-fashioned uniform. There are also reports of another nurse who either jumped or was pushed from the window of Room 502, adding to the room's haunted reputation.

The fourth floor of Waverly Hills is particularly notorious for paranormal activity. Shadow figures, often described as dark, humanoid shapes, are frequently seen darting in and out of rooms and down the hallways. These shadow figures are believed to be the spirits of former patients or staff, their identities lost to history. The oppressive atmosphere on the fourth floor is palpable, with many visitors reporting feelings of unease, cold spots, and the sensation of being watched. Disembodied voices, laughter, and cries for help are also commonly heard in this area of the sanatorium.

One of the most chilling stories associated with Waverly Hills is that of the "Creeper," a malevolent entity that is said to crawl along the floors, walls, and ceilings of the building. Descriptions of the Creeper vary, but it is often depicted as a dark, shadowy figure with an unnerving, spider-like movement. Some believe that the Creeper is a manifestation of the negative energy and suffering that permeated the sanatorium, while others think it may be a demonic presence. Encounters with the Creeper are said to evoke intense fear and dread, even among seasoned paranormal investigators.

The fifth floor of Waverly Hills, particularly Room 502, continues to draw significant attention from those interested in the paranormal. In addition to the suicides associated with this room, it is also rumored to have been the site of cruel and unusual treatments, adding to the dark energy that many feel there. Some visitors have reported being touched or scratched by unseen hands, while others have experienced sudden drops in temperature or the feeling of an invisible presence pressing down on them.

Paranormal investigations at Waverly Hills have yielded a wealth of evidence supporting claims of supernatural activity. Investigators have captured numerous EVPs (Electronic Voice Phenomena), with recordings of disembodied voices responding to questions or making statements. Photographs and videos have also revealed unexplained anomalies, such as orbs of light, shadowy figures, and apparitions. Motion sensors and other detection equipment have picked up movement in empty rooms and hallways, adding to the body of evidence suggesting that Waverly Hills is indeed haunted.

The sanatorium has been featured on numerous television shows and documentaries about haunted locations, including "Ghost Hunters," "Ghost Adventures," and "Destination Fear." These programs have brought Waverly Hills into the spotlight, showcasing its haunted reputation to a global audience. The combination of historical tragedy, eerie architecture, and compelling paranormal evidence makes Waverly Hills a perennial favorite among ghost hunters and enthusiasts.

In addition to its haunted reputation, Waverly Hills is also a significant historical landmark. The building is an example of early 20th-century hospital architecture, designed to maximize airflow and sunlight, which were believed to be beneficial for tuberculosis patients. Despite its dilapidated state, the sanatorium retains much of its original structure and features, providing a glimpse into the past and the challenges of treating a deadly disease before the advent of antibiotics.

Efforts to preserve and restore Waverly Hills are ongoing, led by private owners and historical preservation groups. The sanatorium hosts regular tours and paranormal investigations, which help fund its maintenance and restoration. These events attract thousands of visitors each year, drawn by the opportunity to explore one of America's most haunted locations and to possibly experience its ghostly phenomena firsthand.

The legacy of Waverly Hills Sanatorium is a complex tapestry of history, tragedy, and the supernatural. The ghosts of Waverly Hills are a testament to the countless lives affected by tuberculosis and the harsh treatments endured by patients. They are also a reflection of the intense emotional and physical suffering that took place within its walls.

Whether one believes in ghosts or not, the stories of Waverly Hills serve as a poignant reminder of a dark chapter in medical history and the enduring impact of human suffering.

Chapter 44: The Legend of the Banshee

The legend of the Banshee is one of the most enduring and chilling tales from Irish folklore, a story that has captivated the imaginations of people for centuries. Originating in ancient Celtic traditions, the Banshee, or "bean sí" in Gaelic, is often depicted as a supernatural entity whose wail or keening is believed to foretell the imminent death of a loved one. This mournful cry, described as a mix between a high-pitched wail and a lament, is said to be so sorrowful and chilling that it can freeze the blood of those who hear it.

The Banshee is usually envisioned as a female spirit, though her appearance can vary significantly depending on the region and the storyteller. In some accounts, she is portrayed as an old woman with long, flowing gray hair, a deathly pallor, and eyes red from weeping. Her clothing can be a simple gray or white dress, often ragged and torn, which adds to her spectral appearance. In other variations, the Banshee may appear as a beautiful young woman, her hair a cascading waterfall of red or gold, her clothes immaculate and white as snow. Regardless of her form, the Banshee's most distinguishing feature is her voice, which carries a supernatural quality that is both enchanting and terrifying.

The origins of the Banshee legend are deeply rooted in the historical and cultural fabric of Ireland. Some scholars trace her origins to the ancient practice of keening, where women known as keeners would sing lamentations at funerals. These professional mourners were believed to possess a deep connection to the spiritual world, and their wailing was thought to guide the souls of the dead to the afterlife. Over time, these keeners became conflated with the figure of the Banshee, transforming from mortal mourners into ethereal harbingers of death.

In many stories, the Banshee is not a malicious spirit but rather a sorrowful one. She does not cause death; instead, she serves as a warning, a compassionate figure who mourns the impending loss alongside the bereaved family. Her cry is said to be heard only by those whose family members are destined to die soon, often giving them time to prepare for the inevitable. The Banshee is particularly associated with certain Irish families, particularly those whose surnames begin with O' or Mac, such as the O'Briens, the O'Connors, the MacMahons, and the MacCarthys. These families were considered to have a special connection to the Banshee, who would appear to them in times of impending death as a sign of their ancient lineage and noble heritage.

The Banshee's wail is described in various ways, depending on the region and the teller of the tale. In some accounts, it is a low, mournful moan, while in others it is a piercing scream that can shatter glass. There are even stories where the Banshee's cry is so powerful that it can be heard across great distances, carrying on the wind to reach those who need to hear it. The nature of the Banshee's cry often reflects the nature of the death it portends; a gentle, almost musical lament might signal a peaceful passing, while a blood-curdling shriek might indicate a sudden or violent end.

Encounters with the Banshee are said to be deeply unsettling experiences. Those who have claimed to hear her wail often describe an overwhelming sense of dread and sorrow, as if the very essence of death has brushed against their soul. Some stories recount individuals seeing the Banshee before hearing her cry, often glimpsing her ghostly form at a distance, standing by a river or near the family home. These sightings add to the ominous atmosphere surrounding the Banshee, as her presence alone is enough to send shivers down the spine of even the bravest individuals.

Interestingly, the Banshee legend is not confined to Ireland alone. Variations of the Banshee can be found in Scottish, Welsh, and even American folklore, brought over by Irish immigrants who carried their stories with them to the New World. In Scotland, the Banshee is known as the Bean Nighe, a washerwoman who is seen washing the bloodstained clothes of those who are about to die. This version of the legend emphasizes the Banshee's role as a mourner and a symbol of impending death. In Wales, the spirit is known as the Cyoeraeth, a ghostly figure whose shriek is a sign of death. The spread of the Banshee legend across different cultures underscores the universal human fascination with death and the afterlife, as well as the deep-seated need to find meaning in the face of mortality.

Modern interpretations of the Banshee have kept the legend alive in popular culture. She has appeared in numerous books, movies, and television shows, often depicted as a fearsome and vengeful spirit. However, these portrayals often miss the more nuanced and compassionate aspects of the original legend. The Banshee is not merely a ghostly figure meant to scare, but a complex symbol of mourning, loss, and the enduring connection between the living and the dead. Her story serves as a reminder of the inevitability of death and the importance of family ties, even beyond the grave.

Despite the modernization of the Banshee legend, the core elements remain the same, and her story continues to captivate those who hear it. The Banshee's mournful cry, her ghostly appearance, and her role as a harbinger of death all contribute to her enduring place in the pantheon of supernatural folklore. For many, the legend of the Banshee is more than just a scary story; it is a reflection of the deep cultural and spiritual beliefs of the Irish people, a testament to their reverence for the dead and their understanding of the thin veil that separates this world from the next.

In contemporary times, the legend of the Banshee serves as a cultural touchstone, a way for people to connect with their heritage and explore the mysteries of life and death. While skeptics may dismiss the Banshee as mere myth, those who have experienced her presence or heard her wail often speak of her with a mix of fear and respect. The Banshee's legend, like many other tales of the supernatural, offers a way to confront the unknown, to give form to our deepest fears and hopes about what lies beyond the veil of mortality. Whether one believes in the Banshee as a literal entity or sees her as a metaphorical representation of grief and loss, her story continues to resonate, a haunting reminder of the fragile nature of life and the enduring power of myth.

172

Chapter 45: The Ghost of Kate Morgan

The story of the ghost of Kate Morgan at the Hotel del Coronado is one of the most intriguing and enduring ghost stories in American folklore. The Hotel del Coronado, an iconic and historic beachfront hotel in Coronado, California, has long been associated with tales of hauntings and paranormal activity, but none is more famous than the legend of Kate Morgan, a young woman whose tragic death in the late 19th century has led to countless reports of ghostly encounters and strange occurrences.

Kate Morgan, born Kate Farmer, was a beautiful and enigmatic woman who led a life filled with mystery and misfortune. She married Tom Morgan, a gambler, and the couple traveled extensively. Their relationship was tumultuous, marked by Tom's frequent absences and Kate's increasing despondency. In November 1892, Kate checked into the Hotel del Coronado alone, registering under the name "Lottie A. Bernard." She claimed to be waiting for her brother, a doctor, who was supposed to arrive and treat her for stomach cancer. Over the next five days, hotel staff noted that Kate appeared ill and melancholic. She was often seen walking along the beach, lost in thought.

On the evening of November 28, 1892, Kate was found dead on an exterior staircase leading to the beach. She had a gunshot wound to her head, and a handgun was found near her body. The initial investigation concluded that her death was a suicide, but there were several inconsistencies and unanswered questions that fueled speculation and rumors. The autopsy revealed that the bullet did not match the caliber of the weapon found at the scene, leading some to believe that she might have been murdered. However, no conclusive evidence was ever found to support this theory, and Kate's death was officially ruled a suicide.

The tragic story of Kate Morgan did not end with her death. Almost immediately, guests and staff at the Hotel del Coronado began reporting strange and unexplained occurrences. People claimed to see a young woman in a black dress wandering the halls, disappearing around corners, and walking along the beach at night. This apparition, believed to be the ghost of Kate Morgan, has become one of the hotel's most enduring legends. Room 3327, where Kate stayed during her final days, is said to be the epicenter of the paranormal activity. Guests who have stayed in this room have reported a variety of strange phenomena, including flickering lights, sudden changes in temperature, and the feeling of an unseen presence. Some have even claimed to see Kate's ghostly figure standing by the window or sitting on the edge of the bed.

Over the years, the legend of Kate Morgan has grown, with countless stories and sightings adding to the mystique of the Hotel del Coronado. The hotel's staff has embraced the legend, often sharing the story with curious guests and conducting ghost tours that highlight the most famous hauntings. Despite the commercialization of the ghost story, many people who have experienced the paranormal activity at the hotel remain convinced that Kate Morgan's spirit still lingers, unable to find peace.

One of the most compelling aspects of the Kate Morgan legend is the number of credible witnesses who have reported encounters with her ghost. These include not only guests but also hotel employees, maintenance workers, and security personnel. The consistency of the reports, spanning over a century, adds a layer of credibility to the claims. For example, many witnesses describe the same details: a young woman with long dark hair, dressed in late 19th-century clothing, who appears and vanishes without a trace. The recurring nature of these sightings has intrigued paranormal investigators and skeptics alike.

Several paranormal investigations have been conducted at the Hotel del Coronado, with varying results. Some investigators have captured unexplained phenomena on camera, including orbs of light, strange shadows, and eerie sounds. Others have recorded fluctuations in electromagnetic fields and sudden drops in temperature, both of which are often associated with ghostly activity. These findings, while not definitive proof of the supernatural, have added to the legend and attracted even more attention to the story of Kate Morgan.

One notable investigation was conducted by the team from the television show "Ghost Adventures." They spent several nights at the hotel, using a variety of high-tech equipment to try to capture evidence of paranormal activity. During their investigation, they reported several unexplained occurrences, including disembodied voices, moving objects, and anomalous readings on their instruments. While some skeptics argue that these findings can be explained by natural phenomena or equipment malfunctions, others believe they are proof that Kate Morgan's spirit remains at the Hotel del Coronado.

The historical records surrounding Kate Morgan's life and death also add to the intrigue. Newspaper articles from the time of her death provide a glimpse into the sensationalism and speculation that surrounded the case. Headlines like "Mysterious Death at the Hotel del Coronado" and "Was It Suicide or Murder?" captured the public's imagination and fueled the ghost story that would follow. Over the years, researchers have uncovered more details about Kate's life, including her troubled marriage and her husband's criminal activities, which add layers of complexity to the story.

Despite the passage of time, the ghost of Kate Morgan continues to be a focal point for those interested in the paranormal. Her story is not just a ghost tale but also a tragic narrative of a young woman whose life was cut short under mysterious circumstances. The unanswered questions about her death and the numerous reports of her ghostly presence have ensured that her legend endures. For many, the Hotel del Coronado is not just a luxurious historic hotel but a place where the past and present intersect in the most mysterious of ways.

Visitors to the hotel often seek out Room 3327, hoping to experience something otherworldly. While not everyone leaves with a ghost story, many come away with a deeper appreciation for the history and mystery of the place. The hotel's grand architecture, combined with the eerie tales of hauntings, creates an atmosphere that is both enchanting and unsettling. Whether one believes in ghosts or not, the story of Kate Morgan at the Hotel del Coronado is a reminder of how the past can leave an indelible mark on a place, and how some stories, no matter how old, continue to captivate and intrigue us.

Chapter 46: The Curse of the Crying Boy Paintings

The Curse of the Crying Boy paintings is one of the most unusual and mysterious legends to emerge in the late 20th century, captivating public imagination with tales of inexplicable disasters and supernatural curses. This story revolves around a series of prints and paintings depicting a young boy with an expression of sorrow and tears streaming down his cheeks. These paintings, often referred to collectively as "The Crying Boy," became popular in the 1950s and 1960s, mass-produced and widely sold in the United Kingdom and beyond. The artist behind these haunting images is often identified as Bruno Amadio, also known by his pseudonym Giovanni Bragolin, though there are other artists who created similar works.

The legend of the curse began in the 1980s when British tabloid The Sun published a sensational story about the paintings. On September 4, 1985, the newspaper ran an article under the headline "Blazing Curse of the Crying Boy," recounting the experiences of Ron and May Hall, a couple from Rotherham, South Yorkshire. According to the report, the Halls' home was destroyed by a fire, but remarkably, a framed print of The Crying Boy remained unscathed amidst the charred ruins. The fire brigade claimed they had encountered numerous instances where homes with Crying Boy prints had burned down, yet the prints themselves had survived untouched. This inexplicable phenomenon led to the belief that the paintings were cursed.

Following the publication of the story, many readers came forward with their own tales of misfortune linked to The Crying Boy paintings. Reports poured in from all over the UK, detailing house fires, accidents, and other calamities that seemingly struck those who owned the paintings. These accounts added fuel to the fire, and the legend of the cursed paintings quickly spread. The Sun capitalized on the public's fascination, publishing more articles and even organizing mass burnings of the prints, urging readers to send their Crying Boy paintings to be destroyed to lift the supposed curse.

The origin of the curse is steeped in various rumors and myths. One of the most persistent stories is that the boy depicted in the paintings was an orphan named Don Bonillo, whose parents had perished in a fire. According to this tale, wherever the boy went, a mysterious fire would break out, leading to his nickname "Diablo" or "the Devil." Eventually, the boy himself died in a fire, and his spirit became trapped in the paintings, cursing anyone who possessed them. Another version suggests that the artist, Bruno Amadio, captured the boy's sorrowful expression after witnessing his family die in a blaze, imbuing the paintings with a tragic, supernatural energy.

Skeptics, however, offer more rational explanations for the phenomenon. One theory posits that the prints, made on high-quality, fire-retardant paper, were simply more resistant to fire than other materials, which could explain why they often survived blazes that destroyed everything else. Additionally, the mass production of these prints meant that they were present in many homes, increasing the likelihood of their involvement in coincidental fires. Some fire officials suggested that the string used to hang the prints might have burned through quickly, causing the paintings to fall face down and thus be protected from the flames.

Despite these logical explanations, the legend of the Crying Boy curse persists. The story taps into a primal fear of the unknown and the belief in supernatural forces that can influence our lives in inexplicable ways. The paintings themselves, with their haunting, sorrowful expressions, seem to evoke a sense of unease and mystery that lends credence to the idea of a curse. The widespread media coverage, along with the dramatic narrative of cursed objects causing misfortune, ensured that the legend would endure in popular culture.

Over the years, the Crying Boy paintings have inspired numerous investigations and analyses. Paranormal enthusiasts and researchers have examined the phenomenon, with some conducting experiments to test the fire-retardant properties of the prints. In one famous experiment, conducted by British television show "Ghosthunters" in the 1990s, a Crying Boy print was subjected to direct flames and was observed to resist burning for a significant amount of time. While this did not prove the existence of a curse, it added an intriguing element to the mystery.

The Crying Boy curse has also found its way into literature, film, and television. The paintings have been featured in horror stories, documentaries, and even in episodes of paranormal investigation shows. These portrayals often emphasize the eerie and unsettling nature of the paintings, reinforcing their association with misfortune and the supernatural. The legend has become a part of the broader cultural tapestry of haunted objects and cursed artifacts, akin to tales of cursed jewels, haunted dolls, and other items believed to carry malevolent energies.

In recent years, the Crying Boy paintings have become collectors' items for those fascinated by the paranormal and the macabre. Some collectors seek them out specifically because of the curse, viewing them as intriguing curiosities that add an element of mystery and danger to their collections. For others, the paintings are reminders of a peculiar chapter in modern folklore, a testament to the enduring power of urban legends and the human tendency to find meaning in coincidence and tragedy.

Despite the fear and superstition surrounding the Crying Boy paintings, there are also those who see them as symbols of resilience and survival. The image of the tearful child, often untouched by the flames that consume everything else, can be interpreted as a poignant metaphor for enduring sorrow and loss. This perspective offers a more hopeful interpretation of the legend, suggesting that even in the face of disaster, there can be elements of beauty and strength that remain unscathed.

Ultimately, the story of the Crying Boy curse is a complex and multifaceted legend that continues to captivate and intrigue. Whether viewed as a cautionary tale about the power of superstition, a case study in mass hysteria, or a genuine paranormal mystery, it reflects the enduring human fascination with the unknown and the inexplicable. The Crying Boy paintings, with their haunting expressions and enigmatic backstory, will likely remain a topic of fascination and debate for years to come, a haunting reminder of the thin line between the mundane and the mysterious.

Chapter 47: The Haunted Elvey Farm

Elvey Farm, nestled in the picturesque village of Pluckley in Kent, England, is often described as one of the most haunted locations in the United Kingdom. This historic farmhouse, with origins dating back to the 16th century, is part of the larger narrative of Pluckley, which is frequently cited as England's most haunted village. The farm and its surrounding area are steeped in history, and over the centuries, numerous ghostly legends and paranormal occurrences have been reported, making Elvey Farm a focal point for those fascinated by the supernatural.

Elvey Farm's long and storied history begins in the 16th century, when it was originally built as a working farm. The farmhouse itself is a classic example of Kentish architecture, featuring timber-framed structures and traditional thatched roofs. Throughout its history, the farm has seen a variety of uses, including serving as a family home, a bed and breakfast, and a working farm. The rich history and the many lives that have passed through its doors have undoubtedly contributed to the layers of stories and legends associated with the property.

One of the most famous ghost stories associated with Elvey Farm is that of the "Frightened Cavalier." This spectral figure is said to be the ghost of a Royalist soldier who sought refuge at the farm during the English Civil War in the mid-17th century. According to the legend, the soldier was hiding from Parliamentarian forces when he was discovered and killed. His restless spirit is said to wander the grounds of the farm, often seen wearing period clothing, including a distinctive plumed hat. Witnesses have reported seeing the Frightened Cavalier in various parts of the farm, sometimes appearing in the dead of night, and at other times in broad daylight.

Another prominent ghostly figure at Elvey Farm is the "Monk of the Cellar." This apparition is believed to be the spirit of a monk who lived at the farm during the Middle Ages, when it was part of a larger monastic community. The monk is said to be a benign presence, often seen in the cellar or the lower parts of the farmhouse. Some believe that he is performing penance for some long-forgotten sin, while others suggest that he is simply carrying on his duties from beyond the grave. Sightings of the monk often describe him as a shadowy figure, cloaked in a dark robe, sometimes heard muttering prayers or chanting in Latin.

Elvey Farm is also said to be haunted by the ghost of a young woman known as the "White Lady." This tragic figure is believed to be the spirit of a woman who died under mysterious circumstances on the farm. According to local lore, she was a maid who worked at the farm and fell in love with the farmer's son. Their love was forbidden, and when their affair was discovered, she was driven to despair and took her own life. The White Lady is often seen wandering the halls and grounds of the farm, her spectral form dressed in a flowing white gown. Witnesses have reported feeling an overwhelming sense of sadness and despair when encountering her ghost, as if they are experiencing her heartbreak and sorrow firsthand.

In addition to these well-known apparitions, Elvey Farm is also the site of numerous other paranormal phenomena. Guests and residents have reported hearing disembodied voices, footsteps, and the sounds of doors opening and closing on their own. There are also accounts of objects moving by themselves, sudden drops in temperature, and strange lights appearing in the night sky above the farm. These occurrences have been documented by numerous paranormal investigators who have visited the farm over the years, adding to its reputation as a hotbed of supernatural activity.

One particularly chilling story involves the "Red Lady," a spectral figure believed to be the ghost of a woman who died in childbirth. According to the legend, the woman was buried in a local churchyard with her stillborn child, but her spirit was unable to rest. She is often seen searching for her lost child, her form bathed in a red, ethereal glow. Sightings of the Red Lady are often accompanied by an overwhelming sense of sorrow and loss, and those who have encountered her report feeling a deep, inexplicable sadness.

The village of Pluckley, where Elvey Farm is located, is itself renowned for its numerous ghost stories. The village is said to be home to at least twelve distinct ghosts, each with their own tragic and eerie tale. These include the Screaming Man, believed to be the ghost of a bricklayer who fell to his death while working on a local house, and the Highwayman, the ghost of a notorious robber who was killed by villagers and nailed to a tree. The collective hauntings of Pluckley, including those at Elvey Farm, have made the village a popular destination for ghost hunters and paranormal enthusiasts from around the world.

Despite its reputation for hauntings, Elvey Farm has remained a popular and cherished location. Its rustic charm and historical significance make it an attractive destination for tourists and history buffs alike. The farmhouse has been meticulously preserved and renovated, offering a glimpse into the past while providing modern comforts. Visitors to the farm can stay in its well-appointed guest rooms, dine in its restaurant, and explore the beautiful countryside that surrounds it. For those interested in the paranormal, the farm offers ghost tours and events, providing an opportunity to experience its haunted history firsthand.

The owners and staff of Elvey Farm have embraced its haunted reputation, often sharing their own experiences and those of past guests. They recount tales of strange occurrences, from hearing inexplicable noises in the dead of night to witnessing ghostly apparitions in the corridors. These stories, passed down through generations, have become an integral part of the farm's identity, adding to its allure and mystique.

Paranormal investigators who have studied Elvey Farm often highlight the high level of activity and the variety of phenomena reported. Some investigators have captured compelling evidence, including photographs of orbs and apparitions, EVP (electronic voice phenomenon) recordings of disembodied voices, and temperature readings that defy explanation. These findings have been presented in numerous books, documentaries, and television shows, further cementing Elvey Farm's status as one of the most haunted locations in the UK.

Skeptics, of course, offer alternative explanations for the reported phenomena. They suggest that many of the experiences could be attributed to natural causes, such as the creaking of an old house, drafts, and the power of suggestion. However, even the most skeptical visitors often leave with a sense of wonder and intrigue, unable to fully dismiss the possibility that something otherworldly may be at play.

One of the most famous investigations at Elvey Farm was conducted by the team from the television show "Most Haunted." During their visit, the team experienced a number of unexplained events, including sightings of shadowy figures, sudden temperature drops, and objects moving on their own. The episode featuring Elvey Farm remains one of the most popular in the show's history, drawing attention from viewers around the world and sparking renewed interest in the farm's haunted history.

Elvey Farm's haunted reputation has also had a significant impact on the local community. The stories of ghostly encounters have become a part of the village's cultural heritage, passed down through generations and shared with visitors. The farm and the village of Pluckley have become a symbol of the enduring power of folklore and the human fascination with the supernatural. The blend of history, mystery, and the unexplained has created a unique and captivating narrative that continues to draw people to this quaint corner of Kent.

Chapter 48: The Poltergeist of Thornton Heath

The Poltergeist of Thornton Heath is one of the most disturbing and well-documented cases of poltergeist activity in British history. This terrifying series of events, which occurred in the 1970s, gripped the nation and left a lasting impression on those who experienced it firsthand. The haunting took place in a suburban home in Thornton Heath, a town in the London Borough of Croydon. The incidents involved an ordinary family, whose lives were turned upside down by inexplicable and often violent paranormal phenomena.

The story begins in August 1972, when a family, whom we'll call the Harrisons to respect their privacy, started experiencing strange occurrences in their home. It all started innocuously enough with unexplained noises, such as knocking and tapping sounds, that seemed to have no source. At first, the family dismissed these noises as the natural creaks and groans of an old house settling. However, the disturbances soon escalated in both frequency and intensity.

One of the first major incidents occurred late one night when the family was awakened by the sound of loud banging coming from the living room. When Mr. Harrison went to investigate, he found that the furniture had been rearranged, with chairs overturned and objects scattered across the room. There was no sign of forced entry, and no logical explanation for how the furniture had moved on its own. The family was baffled and disturbed by this event, but it was only the beginning of their ordeal.

Over the following weeks, the disturbances grew more aggressive. Objects would fly across the room, often narrowly missing family members. Heavy pieces of furniture would slide across the floor as if pushed by an unseen force. The family reported hearing disembodied voices and seeing shadowy figures flitting about the house. One particularly frightening incident involved the family's pet cat, which was thrown across the room by an invisible force, leaving the animal terrified and the family shaken.

The Harrisons began to feel as though they were under siege in their own home. The poltergeist seemed to target them individually, with each family member experiencing their own terrifying encounters. Mrs. Harrison reported feeling an unseen hand grab her arm, leaving red marks that resembled finger impressions. Their teenage son, Stephen, was thrown from his bed on several occasions, waking up in a state of panic and fear. Even their young daughter, Emma, was not spared, as she would often wake up screaming, claiming to have seen a "scary man" in her room.

In desperation, the Harrisons sought help from various sources. They consulted with local clergy, who performed blessings and exorcisms in an attempt to rid the house of the malevolent presence. Unfortunately, these efforts only seemed to agitate the poltergeist further. They also reached out to paranormal investigators, who conducted a series of investigations and attempted to document the activity. The investigators reported witnessing several phenomena firsthand, including objects moving on their own and sudden drops in temperature.

One of the investigators, a well-known psychic medium named Maurice Grosse, spent several nights in the house. During his stay, he experienced a range of paranormal activities, from unexplained noises to physical attacks. Grosse believed that the poltergeist was an intelligent entity, capable of interacting with its environment and the people within it. He documented his findings in meticulous detail, providing a wealth of evidence for future researchers.

The case of the Thornton Heath poltergeist garnered significant media attention, with newspapers and television programs covering the family's plight. Journalists and curious onlookers would often gather outside the house, hoping to catch a glimpse of the supernatural events.

The increased attention only seemed to exacerbate the family's stress and anxiety, as they struggled to maintain a semblance of normalcy amid the chaos.

One particularly chilling aspect of the haunting was the poltergeist's apparent ability to manipulate electrical devices. Lights would flicker on and off, appliances would turn on by themselves, and the television would change channels without anyone touching the remote. These disturbances added an extra layer of fear and uncertainty, as the family never knew when or how the poltergeist would strike next.

In one of the most dramatic incidents, the family's Christmas tree was violently shaken, causing ornaments to fly off and smash against the walls. This event, witnessed by multiple family members, left them deeply unsettled and convinced that they were dealing with a malevolent force. The poltergeist seemed to have an uncanny ability to manifest at the most inopportune moments, disrupting family gatherings and social events with its terrifying antics.

The psychological toll on the family was immense. They lived in a constant state of fear, never knowing when the next attack would come. The children, in particular, suffered from nightmares and anxiety, their once-happy home transformed into a place of dread. The parents, desperate to protect their family, felt helpless and overwhelmed by the relentless onslaught of paranormal activity.

After enduring months of torment, the Harrisons made the difficult decision to move out of their home. They hoped that by leaving the house, they could escape the poltergeist and regain some semblance of peace. However, the activity did not cease entirely. Reports of poltergeist activity followed them to their new residence, although it was less intense than before. This led some investigators to speculate that the entity might be attached to a family member, rather than the house itself.

In the years since the Thornton Heath poltergeist case, the story has become a part of British paranormal lore. It has been the subject of numerous books, documentaries, and television shows, each offering their own interpretation of the events. Some researchers believe that the activity was the result of psychokinetic energy, possibly generated by the family's stress and emotional turmoil. Others suggest that the poltergeist was a malevolent spirit, intent on causing harm and disruption.

Skeptics, of course, offer alternative explanations. They argue that the disturbances could be attributed to natural phenomena, such as drafts, settling foundations, and electrical malfunctions. They also suggest that some of the events may have been exaggerated or even fabricated, either intentionally or as a result of the family's heightened fear and anxiety. While these explanations may account for some of the phenomena, they do not fully address the sheer volume and intensity of the reported activity.

The Thornton Heath poltergeist case remains a topic of debate and fascination within the paranormal community. It is a stark reminder of the power of the unknown and the profound impact that unexplained phenomena can have on ordinary lives. For the Harrison family, the haunting was a life-changing experience, one that left an indelible mark on their memories and their sense of reality.

In reflecting on the Thornton Heath poltergeist, it is important to consider the broader context of poltergeist activity and its place in the field of paranormal research. Poltergeists, often characterized by their noisy and disruptive behavior, are among the most perplexing and controversial phenomena in the study of the supernatural. Unlike traditional ghosts, which are often thought to be the spirits of deceased individuals, poltergeists are typically associated with physical disturbances and are sometimes believed to be manifestations of repressed human emotions or energies.

The Thornton Heath case fits many of the classic characteristics of a poltergeist haunting: objects moving on their own, loud noises, physical attacks, and an apparent focus on a particular family or individual. These features have been documented in numerous other cases around the world, leading some researchers to propose that poltergeists may represent a distinct category of paranormal phenomena. Theories about the nature of poltergeists vary widely, ranging from spirits or entities with malevolent intent to subconscious psychic projections generated by living individuals.

In the end, the Thornton Heath poltergeist remains an enduring mystery. Despite the numerous investigations, reports, and analyses, there is no definitive explanation for the events that took place in that suburban home in the 1970s. The case continues to captivate the imagination, serving as a powerful example of the strange and unexplainable occurrences that sometimes intrude upon everyday life. For those who experienced it, the haunting was a terrifying ordeal that challenged their understanding of reality and left them forever changed. For the broader public, it is a fascinating story that underscores the enduring allure of the paranormal and the mysteries that lie just beyond the edges of our understanding.

Chapter 49: The Ghost of Flight 401

The Ghost of Flight 401 is one of the most intriguing and chilling stories in the annals of aviation history. This haunting tale involves the ill-fated Eastern Air Lines Flight 401, which crashed into the Florida Everglades on the night of December 29, 1972. The tragic accident resulted in the loss of over 100 lives and left an indelible mark on the survivors, rescuers, and the aviation industry. However, what sets this disaster apart from other aviation tragedies are the numerous reports of ghostly encounters and paranormal phenomena that followed in its wake. These accounts have been meticulously documented and continue to be a topic of fascination for paranormal enthusiasts and researchers alike.

Eastern Air Lines Flight 401 was a Lockheed L-1011 TriStar, a state-of-the-art aircraft at the time, commanded by Captain Robert Loft, a seasoned pilot with thousands of flight hours under his belt. On that fateful night, the plane was en route from New York's John F. Kennedy International Airport to Miami International Airport. The flight proceeded uneventfully until the approach to Miami, when the crew encountered a problem with the landing gear indicator. The indicator light, which was supposed to signal the proper deployment of the landing gear, failed to illuminate.

Concerned about the potential failure of the landing gear, Captain Loft and his crew, which included First Officer Albert Stockstill and Second Officer Donald Repo, began troubleshooting the issue. They decided to enter a holding pattern over the Everglades while they attempted to resolve the problem. During this time, the autopilot was inadvertently disengaged, causing the aircraft to descend unnoticed. The crew, focused on the landing gear indicator, failed to realize their perilous descent until it was too late. At 11:42 PM, Flight 401 crashed into the remote and swampy terrain of the Everglades.

The impact was catastrophic. The plane broke apart, scattering debris and passengers across the marshy landscape. Of the 176 people on board, 101 perished in the crash, including Captain Loft and First Officer Stockstill. Remarkably, 75 passengers and crew members survived, thanks in large part to the quick response of rescuers who braved the treacherous conditions of the Everglades to reach the crash site. Among the survivors was Second Officer Donald Repo, who was severely injured and succumbed to his injuries shortly after the crash.

In the aftermath of the disaster, an investigation by the National Transportation Safety Board (NTSB) concluded that the crash was due to pilot error, primarily the crew's failure to monitor the flight instruments while troubleshooting the landing gear indicator. However, this explanation did little to comfort those who had lost loved ones or the survivors who were haunted by the memories of that night. But it was not just the survivors who were haunted. In the months and years that followed, stories of ghostly encounters began to emerge, centered around the wreckage of Flight 401 and the components salvaged from the crash site.

Eastern Air Lines, in an effort to recoup some of the financial losses from the disaster, salvaged many usable parts from the wreckage of Flight 401. These components, including galley ovens, overhead bins, and other equipment, were refurbished and installed in other L-1011 aircraft in the fleet. It is here that the legend of the Ghost of Flight 401 truly begins. Reports of strange occurrences and ghostly sightings on planes containing parts from Flight 401 became alarmingly frequent.

One of the most commonly reported apparitions was that of Captain Robert Loft. Passengers and crew members on various Eastern Air Lines flights claimed to have seen a man in a pilot's uniform who resembled Loft. These sightings were not limited to brief glimpses; in some cases, the apparition would engage in conversation with the living. Flight attendants reported encountering Loft in the galley, where he would calmly inform them of potential mechanical issues before vanishing. On one occasion, a captain of another flight saw Loft's reflection in the cockpit window, only to turn around and find no one there.

Second Officer Donald Repo was also frequently seen. Repo's ghost was often spotted in the lower galley area, where he had spent much of his time during flights. Flight attendants reported seeing him checking equipment and performing routine tasks. Some even claimed that Repo's ghost would appear to warn them of specific mechanical problems, much like Loft's apparition. In one particularly eerie incident, a flight engineer saw Repo's face in an oven door, accompanied by a voice that urged him to "watch out for fire on this airplane." Shortly thereafter, the aircraft experienced a fire in one of its engines, which was quickly contained.

The stories of Loft and Repo's ghosts were not just the result of overactive imaginations or mass hysteria. These sightings were documented by multiple credible witnesses, including experienced pilots and flight attendants. The consistency of the reports, coupled with the fact that they were made independently of one another, lends a degree of credibility to the accounts. Eastern Air Lines management initially dismissed the reports as nonsense, but as the sightings continued, they became harder to ignore.

The paranormal activity associated with Flight 401 extended beyond visual sightings. There were numerous reports of unexplained noises, such as knocking and banging sounds, emanating from areas of the aircraft where salvaged parts had been installed. Some crew members reported feeling sudden drops in temperature, a common phenomenon associated with ghostly presences. Others experienced feelings of being watched or touched by unseen hands. These disturbances, while unsettling, were often accompanied by a sense of reassurance, as if the spirits of Loft and Repo were watching over the flights and ensuring their safety.

The haunted reputation of the planes containing parts from Flight 401 eventually became too much for Eastern Air Lines to ignore. The airline conducted an internal investigation and, although no official explanation was provided, many of the salvaged components were quietly removed from the fleet. Despite these efforts, stories of ghostly encounters continued to surface, suggesting that the spirits of Loft and Repo were not bound to the physical parts of the aircraft, but rather to the memory of Flight 401 itself.

The story of the Ghost of Flight 401 has been the subject of numerous books, documentaries, and television programs. One of the most notable accounts is found in the book "The Ghost of Flight 401" by John G. Fuller, published in 1976. Fuller conducted extensive interviews with survivors, witnesses, and Eastern Air Lines personnel, compiling a detailed and compelling narrative of the haunting. The book became a bestseller and helped to cement the legend of Flight 401 in popular culture.

Skeptics, of course, offer alternative explanations for the sightings and phenomena associated with Flight 401. They suggest that the trauma and stress experienced by the survivors and witnesses could have led to hallucinations and misinterpretations of ordinary events. The power of suggestion, coupled with the emotional weight of the tragedy, might have contributed to the proliferation of ghost stories. However, these explanations do not fully account for the consistency and specificity of the reports, nor do they explain the corroborating evidence provided by multiple credible witnesses.

The legacy of Flight 401 and its haunting extends beyond the realm of the supernatural. The crash prompted significant changes in aviation safety protocols and training procedures. The NTSB's investigation highlighted the importance of crew resource management (CRM), a set of training procedures designed to improve communication and coordination among flight crew members. The lessons learned from the crash of Flight 401 have undoubtedly contributed to the overall safety of commercial aviation.

For those who believe in the paranormal, the Ghost of Flight 401 serves as a poignant reminder of the enduring connection between the living and the dead. The spirits of Captain Loft and Second Officer Repo are seen not as malevolent entities, but as guardian spirits, watching over the flights and crews that came after them. Their continued presence is a testament to their dedication and sense of duty, even in the face of death.

Chapter 50: The Ghosts of the Shanghai Tunnels

The Ghosts of the Shanghai Tunnels weave a haunting tale through the underbelly of Portland, Oregon. These tunnels, also known as the Old Portland Underground, are a network of passages and basements that once connected the basements of various hotels and bars to the Willamette River waterfront. The labyrinthine tunnels were constructed in the late 19th century and early 20th century, serving multiple purposes, both mundane and sinister. Their history is deeply intertwined with tales of human trafficking, known as "shanghaiing," where unsuspecting individuals were kidnapped and forced into servitude aboard ships. The dark legacy of these tunnels, combined with their eerie atmosphere, has given rise to numerous reports of paranormal activity.

The term "shanghaiing" refers to the practice of abducting men and women to work on ships bound for East Asia, often Shanghai, hence the name. This nefarious activity was rampant in Portland during the late 1800s and early 1900s, fueled by the city's bustling port and the demand for labor on the high seas. The tunnels provided an ideal means for traffickers to transport their captives from the saloons and hotels to the docks without attracting attention. Victims were often drugged or intoxicated, then dragged through trapdoors in the floors of establishments and into the tunnels below. Once there, they would be held in cells until they could be smuggled onto ships.

The conditions within the Shanghai Tunnels were deplorable. The underground passages were dark, damp, and infested with rats. Captives were often shackled and kept in tiny, cramped cells, with little to no light or ventilation. Many of them were beaten or otherwise mistreated to keep them subdued. The fear and desperation felt by those imprisoned in the tunnels have left an indelible mark on the location, contributing to the area's reputation for paranormal activity.

One of the most commonly reported apparitions in the Shanghai Tunnels is that of a ghostly woman named Nina. According to legend, Nina was a young woman who worked as a prostitute in one of the hotels connected to the tunnels. She is said to have overheard details of the shanghaiing operations and threatened to expose the traffickers. To silence her, she was murdered and her body was hidden in the tunnels. Visitors and tour guides frequently report seeing Nina's apparition, described as a woman in a white dress, wandering the tunnels. Her presence is often accompanied by a feeling of sadness or unease, and some have reported hearing her disembodied voice calling for help.

Another frequently encountered spirit is that of a man known as "Crimp." Crimp was a term used to describe the men who orchestrated the shanghaiing operations, luring victims to their fate. The ghost of Crimp is said to be one of these notorious figures, continuing his sinister work from beyond the grave. Witnesses have reported seeing a shadowy figure lurking in the darker corners of the tunnels, often accompanied by the sound of footsteps or the feeling of being watched. Some believe that Crimp's spirit remains trapped in the tunnels as punishment for his deeds, forever bound to the place where he caused so much suffering.

In addition to these specific apparitions, the Shanghai Tunnels are also home to numerous other paranormal phenomena. Visitors often report experiencing sudden drops in temperature, unexplained cold spots, and the feeling of being touched or brushed by unseen hands. Disembodied voices, ranging from whispers to full-throated cries, are commonly heard echoing through the tunnels. Electronic equipment, such as cameras and flashlights, frequently malfunctions or drains of battery power unexpectedly. These occurrences, while unsettling, have become a significant draw for paranormal investigators and ghost hunters.

One particularly chilling story involves a tour group that was exploring the tunnels when they encountered what appeared to be a solid, human figure standing in the darkness. Assuming it was another member of the group, the guide called out, but received no response. As they approached, the figure simply vanished into thin air, leaving the group shaken and bewildered. Such incidents are not uncommon, with many visitors reporting similar experiences of seeing apparitions that disappear upon closer inspection.

The history of the Shanghai Tunnels is also marked by tragedy and violence outside of the shanghaiing operations. The tunnels were often used by criminals for various illicit activities, including smuggling, gambling, and opium dens. Conflicts between rival gangs and other criminal elements sometimes resulted in violent confrontations, leaving behind a legacy of bloodshed. The energy from these violent events is believed by some to contribute to the tunnels' haunted reputation.

The tunnels also served as a refuge for those seeking to escape the harsh realities of life above ground. During the Prohibition era, the tunnels were used to smuggle alcohol into the city, providing a lifeline for speakeasies and underground bars. These hidden establishments offered a semblance of normalcy and enjoyment during a time of strict prohibition laws. However, the illegal nature of these activities meant that they were often fraught with danger, adding to the tunnels' already dark history.

The Shanghai Tunnels have become a popular destination for ghost tours and paranormal investigations. Organizations such as the Cascade Geographic Society offer guided tours of the tunnels, providing visitors with a glimpse into their haunted history. These tours often include accounts of ghost sightings and other paranormal activity, as well as historical information about the tunnels and their role in Portland's past. The combination of history and hauntings makes the tours both educational and spine-tingling, drawing in those with an interest in the supernatural.

Despite the numerous reports of paranormal activity, some skeptics argue that the haunted reputation of the Shanghai Tunnels is largely the result of overactive imaginations and the power of suggestion. They point out that the dark, claustrophobic environment of the tunnels can easily induce feelings of fear and unease, leading people to interpret natural sounds and occurrences as supernatural. While this may account for some experiences, it does not fully explain the consistency and specificity of many reports.

In recent years, the Shanghai Tunnels have also become the subject of various media productions. Television shows, documentaries, and podcasts have explored the tunnels' haunted history, often featuring interviews with witnesses and paranormal investigators. These programs have helped to popularize the legend of the Shanghai Tunnels, bringing their eerie tales to a wider audience. The stories of ghostly encounters and paranormal phenomena continue to captivate viewers, adding to the mystique of the tunnels.

For those who believe in the paranormal, the Shanghai Tunnels offer compelling evidence of life beyond death. The apparitions, disembodied voices, and unexplained phenomena reported in the tunnels suggest that the spirits of those who suffered and died there remain trapped, unable or unwilling to move on. These spirits may be seeking justice, trying to communicate their stories, or simply reliving their final moments. Whatever their motivations, their presence serves as a haunting reminder of the tunnels' dark past.

Epilogue

As we conclude our journey through the eerie and enigmatic tales of "Documented Paranormal Events," it is clear that the line between the known and the unknown is far more blurred than we might have imagined. From haunted houses to ghost ships, from mysterious creatures to inexplicable phenomena, the stories within these pages remind us that the world is filled with mysteries that defy conventional explanation.

Throughout history, these documented events have left an indelible mark on the lives of those who experienced them, as well as on the communities and cultures that recorded and passed down their stories. They challenge us to look beyond the boundaries of our understanding and to remain open to the possibility that there are aspects of our reality that we have yet to fully comprehend.

The accounts presented here are not mere campfire tales or urban legends; they are documented occurrences backed by eyewitness testimonies, historical records, and, in some cases, physical evidence. They serve as a testament to the resilience of human curiosity and our unending quest to make sense of the world around us.

As you close this book, take a moment to reflect on what you have read. Consider the common threads that run through these diverse stories—fear, wonder, disbelief, and awe. Ask yourself what you believe and why. Are these events simply the result of coincidence and misinterpretation, or do they point to something deeper, something that exists just beyond the reach of our current scientific understanding?

In the end, the true value of these stories lies not in proving or disproving their authenticity but in their ability to ignite our imagination and provoke thoughtful inquiry. They remind us that the universe is vast and mysterious, and that there is still so much to learn and discover.

May these tales inspire you to look at the world with fresh eyes, to question the ordinary, and to embrace the extraordinary. Remember that the unknown is not something to be feared but something to be explored and understood. Whether you remain a skeptic, become a believer, or find yourself somewhere in between, let the stories of "Documented Paranormal Events" stay with you as a reminder that the world is full of wonders waiting to be uncovered.

Thank you for joining me on this journey into the unknown. The stories may have ended, but the mystery continues.

The End.